The Figure in Action

Marble sculpture 'Els Primers freds',
138 × 100 × 73 cm, by Miquel Blay.
Museum of Modern Art, Barcelona

THE FIGURE IN ACTION

Anatomy for Artists

Louise Gordon

B T BATSFORD LIMITED LONDON

To dear Ruth and Kenneth

First published 1989
Reprinted 1991, 1992, 1995, 1997

Typeset by Servis Filmsetting Limited, Manchester
and printed in Great Britain by
Bath Press, Bath
for the publishers
B T Batsford Limited
583 Fulham Road
London SW6 5BY

ISBN 0 7134 5946 8 (hardback)

ISBN 0 7134 5947 6 (paperback)

Contents

Acknowledgment

My thanks are extended to the publishers and especially to Thelma Nye, senior editor at Batsford, and to my husband Andrew Ramsden Cooper for his infinite patience, wit and wisdom. I would also like to express my gratitude to five teachers: Elwood O Simpson, Maria T Wishart who started the Art as Applied to Medicine course in Canada, Dr JCB Grant, Professor of Anatomy and Dr A W Ham, Professor of Histology with whom I was fortunate to be a student at the University of Toronto Medical School, and Fred Hagan, Ontario College of Art. And also Dr John Basmajian, Professor of Anatomy.

Louise Gordon, 1989

The author

Louise Gordon BA, Dip Medical Illustration, Canadian Academy of Medical Illustrators, AOCA, is a graduate of Toronto Teachers' College, of Queen's University, Kingston, Ontario, of the University of Toronto in Medical Illustration, and of the Ontario College of Art (sculpture). She was lecturer and staff artist at the University of Toronto and medical artist at Sunnybrook Veterans' Hospital, Toronto, for 13 years. She also worked as a free lance artist on several of the leading medical text books in Anatomy, Surgery, and Histology.

For some years she has worked in fine art, and taught Anatomy and Life Drawing at the Sir John Cass College of Art, London, England. She is the author of *Drawing the Human Head*, and *Anatomy and Figure Drawing* also published by Batsford.

Preface

This book considers the body as a whole in both subtle and extreme action. The skeletal structures and the muscle forms are closely related in the drawings to the forms one sees on the surface. Wherever possible the landmarks are shown where bones give form on the surface, to help either for quick sketching, or more developed drawings, paintings, or sculptures.

For more precise anatomical information, a definite line is used to delineate the figures in the drawings. This is useful for outline pattern drawing and for the use of the line brought within the figure to show the form. For those interested in creating the illusion of a solid form in space, a hard line on the edge can sometimes deny the continuation of that form. For sculptors, the whole surface is an edge at times as the form is being developed in the round, reflecting and losing light.

Foremost in the consciousness should be the fact that what one sees and interprets is light being reflected from a surface. It becomes necessary then to look at the gradations of shadow as the form recedes from the light, and for painters to observe the colour changes.

Sometimes the lighting will be such that a part of the body will merge with the background completely, because of colour juxtaposition or an identical tonal effect. Then it is decision time for expressing what you see, or what you know is there, or combining them. At such times an abstraction can emerge, and be developed as a form continuous with its environment. In this context those meanings of the word *abstract* are: to consider, apart from the concrete, something visionary, a negation of one or more objects in consequence of the mind's concentration on another.

The racial and sexual differences are purposely not referred to in this book as it seems more helpful to look at each subject in its uniqueness. Stable landmarks which we all have in common seem better than shifting rules.

More detailed anatomical information and drawing techniques are contained in my previous books, *Drawing the Human Head*, and *Anatomy and Figure Drawing* also published by Batsford.

Hove, East Sussex 1989   LG

Muscle structure and action

The two components of skeletal muscle are a fleshy part composed of muscle cells and a fibrous part called a tendon or aponeurosis. Tendons are usually round and cord-like or flat bands. They are designed for strength, consisting mainly of protein fibres called collagen which lie longitudinally in the muscle axis, and are plaited. There are also a low percentage of elastic fibres which allow for about 4 per cent contraction. When a tendon needs a wide area of attachment it becomes sheet-like and is then called an aponeurosis. The collagen fibres extend into the bone which results in extra bone growth being stimulated in these areas called tubercles, tuberosities, and processes.

Muscle cells are arranged into bundles of many cells and these bundles can shorten to about one half their length. Muscle cells are specialized to perform one function, and that is to contract. When the bundles shorten they therefore become thicker. When they thicken the form on the surface will bulge more, which they do when a muscle is producing action. All the bundles of a muscle do not have to act at one time. This explains why a slow change of form may be seen on the surface as more and more cells are stimulated into contraction to provide the action demanded.

Muscles have different arrangements of their cell bundles and also their tendons according to the demands of the power expected. Bundles of cells are arranged in long parallels if the action is to be maintained through a long distance. If greater power is needed, the muscle bundles are arranged in short diagonal bundles with far more numerous cells.

Muscles act on the skeleton to move it because they span joints. The usual plan is that the fleshy part is attached by fibres to one bone, and the tendon of this muscle spans a joint and inserts into another bone. There is also the design where the fleshy part is in the middle and tendons on either end span a joint. When the fleshy part contracts, the bone, which is the more movable, is drawn toward the other bone.

There is an exception in the face apart from the two muscles which control the jaw joint. Muscles of the face have two different designs: circular muscles which surround the eyes and the mouth openings, and long muscles whose muscle bundles interweave at the edges of the circular ones, and pull on the circular ones when they contract. There are also muscles which attach to the skin and move it and cause puckering.

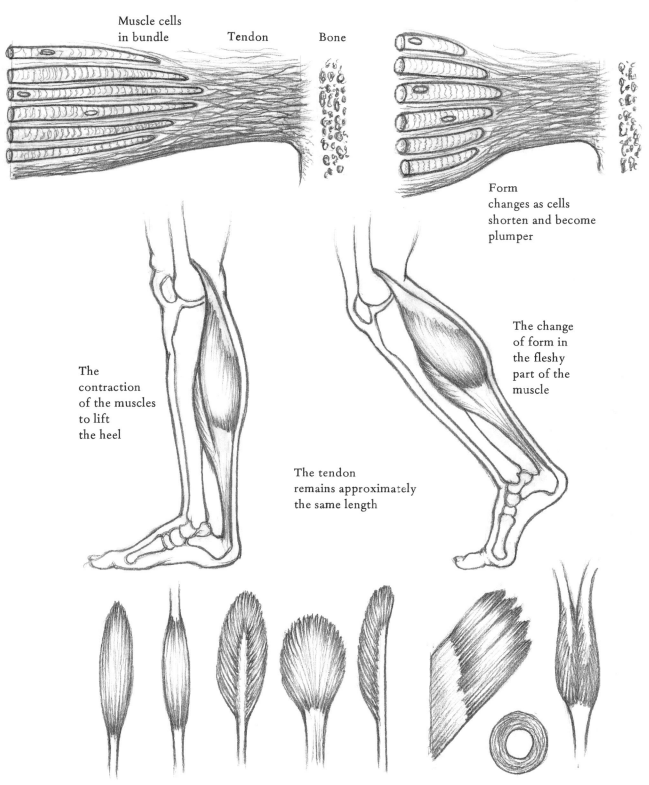

Muscle cells in bundle

Tendon

Bone

Form changes as cells shorten and become plumper

The contraction of the muscles to lift the heel

The change of form in the fleshy part of the muscle

The tendon remains approximately the same length

The fleshy part and tendons take different forms according to the attachment possible, the movement and power needed

9

The muscles of the face and their actions

There are two main muscles of the face. ORBICULARIS OCULI encircles the eye and ORBICULARIS ORIS encircles the mouth. They are called sphincters because when they contract they close an opening.

The other muscles of the face which are interwoven into the edges of these two muscles, when they contract, pull on them and create action and the expression of the face. These muscles are:

FRONTALIS which covers the frontal bone. When it contracts it pulls up orbicularis oculi and creates the horizontal frown lines on the forehead.

LEVATOR LABII ALAEQUE NASI (levator-lift, labii-lip, alaeque-wing, nasi-nose), lifts the upper lip.

LEVATOR LABII interweaves with orbicularis oris. It lifts the lip.

LEVATOR ANGULI ORIS lifts the corner of the mouth.

ZYGOMATICUS MINOR and ZYGOMATICUS MAJOR lift the corner of the mouth and are called the 'smiling muscles'.

RISORIUS, attaching to the parotid gland, pulls horizontally on the corner of the mouth and is called the 'grinning muscle'.

DEPRESSOR LABII pulls the lip down.

DEPRESSOR ANGULI ORIS pull the corner of the mouth down.

There are also two muscles attached to the skin:

CORRUGATOR, arising from the frontal bone, its muscle bundles pass up through frontalis muscle to attach to the skin. They cause the frowning furrows at the top of the nose when they contract.

The MENTALES, a pair of cone-shaped muscles whose apices are attached to the front of the jaw and whose muscle bundles are attached to the skin of the chin. They can be felt as two round forms. A dimple in the chin is an indentation between two cones. The mentales move and pucker the skin in this area.

Note: These muscles are considered in detail with the facial expressions resulting from their contractions in, *Drawing The Human Head* by Louise Gordon, Batsford paperback 1985.

Muscles of the face

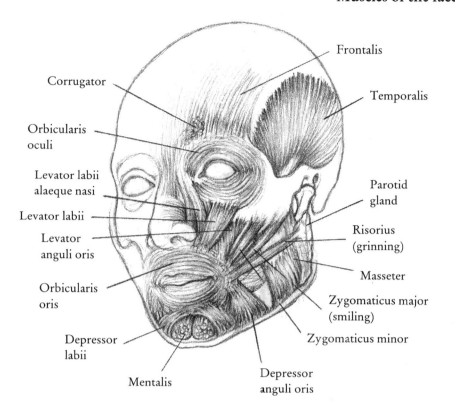

Corrugator

Orbicularis
oculi

Levator labii
alaeque nasi

Levator labii

Levator
anguli oris

Orbicularis
oris

Depressor
labii

Mentalis

Frontalis

Temporalis

Parotid
gland

Risorius
(grinning)

Masseter

Zygomaticus major
(smiling)

Zygomaticus minor

Depressor
anguli oris

The bones of the skull

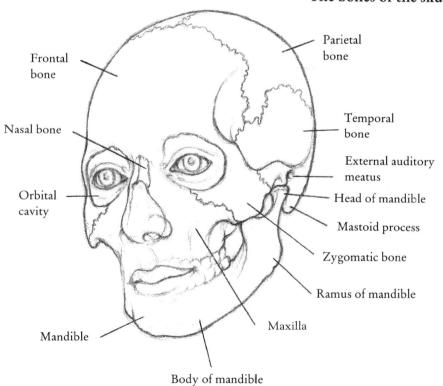

Frontal
bone

Nasal bone

Orbital
cavity

Mandible

Body of mandible

Parietal
bone

Temporal
bone

External auditory
meatus

Head of mandible

Mastoid process

Zygomatic bone

Ramus of mandible

Maxilla

Structures concerning the eyes and their actions

The eyeball lies protected within the anterior half of the cone of bone, the orbital cavity. The eyelids also protect it, especially the upper one. This position in the skull places the eyes in the front plane of the head.

The eyeball is about 25 mm in diameter, the white part called the sclera making up five-sixths of the ball. The anterior one-sixth is the transparent cornea which projects like a little dome. Behind the cornea is the flat disc called the iris. This is composed of muscle tissue which can contract to close and also open the pupil, which is the hole in the iris which allows light to enter. Radial bundles of muscle cells open it, and these striations are visible, and there are also muscle bundles running circularly around the pupil forming a sphincter.

The orbital cavity is filled in its posterior half by the optic nerve, fat, the muscles which control eye movements, and the vessels and nerves. The fat serves to cushion the eye if it is struck. In an emaciated person with fat depletion, the eye will sink in the orbit.

The eyelids are composed of soft tissue which take the form to a great extent of the eyeball under them. The upper lid is capable of much greater movement. The muscle which turns the eyeball upward, the superior rectus, is a laminated section of the muscle to the upper lid, the levator palpebrae. They have the same nerve supply so they work together. The upper lid can also work, under the will, by itself. Also, when the eye looks down the upper lid comes down with it.

General information: The medial canthus (corner) of the eye is usually lower than the lateral canthus so the eye is set on a diagonal which runs downward to the nose. This is to enable the film of tears which bathes the eye constantly to drain into tear ducts which open into the upper and lower lids at the medial canthus.

Note: When drawing the eye it helps greatly if one thinks first of the sphere behind the lids. Then the lids can be put in working over and around that round form.

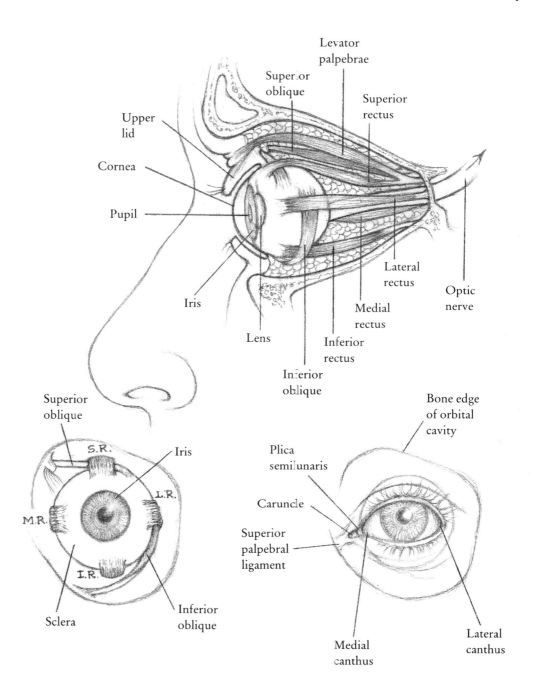

Levator palpebrae

Superior oblique

Superior rectus

Upper lid

Cornea

Pupil

Iris

Lens

Inferior oblique

Inferior rectus

Medial rectus

Lateral rectus

Optic nerve

Superior oblique

S.R.

Iris

L.R.

M.R.

I.R.

Sclera

Inferior oblique

Bone edge of orbital cavity

Plica semilunaris

Caruncle

Superior palpebral ligament

Medial canthus

Lateral canthus

Muscles and actions of the eyes

There are six muscles attached to the ball of the eye which then insert into the bone of the orbital cavity. These muscles are: the SUPERIOR RECTUS, the INFERIOR RECTUS, the MEDIAL RECTUS, the LATERAL RECTUS, the SUPERIOR OBLIQUE and the INFERIOR OBLIQUE. They are responsible for all the actions of the eyes, which work together linked by brain pathways.

For example, to look to the right the LATERAL RECTUS of the right eye and the MEDIAL RECTUS of the left eye are both contracting. The two oblique muscles work with the rectus muscles to give the diagonal movements of the eyes.

In drawing the eye remember that the coloured iris is a flat disc with a hole in it. When a flat disc is turned away from one it becomes an ellipse. When the eyes are turned up or down, or to either side the shape of the iris is always slightly elliptical. Only when a person is looking directly at you is the disc a circle. Also the eyelids have a thickness which can be seen clearly. The upper lid often casts a shadow on the eyeball if the light is falling on the lid.

The eyelids have the contour
of the eyeball to a great
extent and and also their
thickness at their edges can
be seen

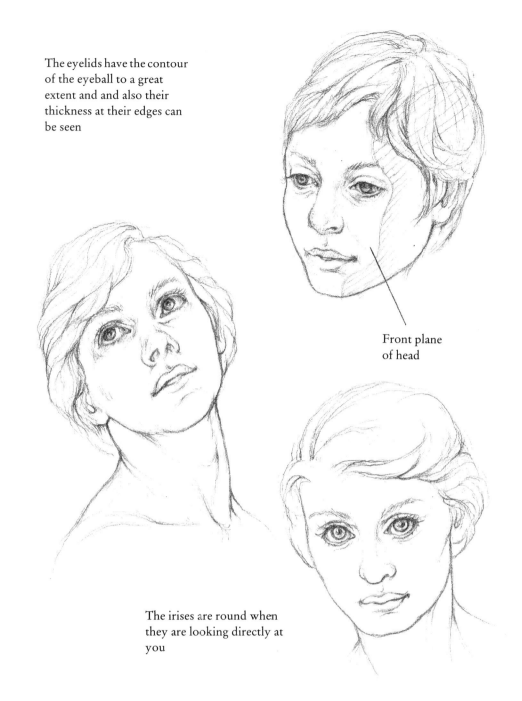

Front plane
of head

The irises are round when
they are looking directly at
you

The front and side of head with neck components

The HYOID BONE is the anchor point for the muscles which open the mouth by pulling the mandible (jaw) down. It is also the attachment point for all but one of the muscles at the front of the neck. It is U-shaped and has a middle, the body, and elongated processes on either side, the lesser and greater horns. It had fibrous attachment to the thyroid cartilage just below it, and thus to the cricoid cartilage and the cartilaginous rings of the trachea (incomplete at the back) which are also joined together by strong fibres. Altogether these form the neck section of the air passage to the lungs. This neck section, especially on thinner necks, is seen as a rounded column and the thyroid cartilage, cricoid cartilage, and the rings of the trachea can at times be seen.

The THYROID CARTILAGE is formed by two plates of cartilage which in development have fused together in an angle at the front to make a V-shaped structure. Posteriorly, the edges are thickened and have small horn projecions above and below. Beneath, and joined to it by both muscle and fibres is the complete ring of the CRICOID CARTILAGE. These two cartilages house the components of the vocal cords.

In the male, the two plates fuse together at a more acute angle than the female. These plates are also larger and therefore make a more prominent structure in the male neck.

In the action of swallowing, the hyoid bone is pulled forward and the thyroid cartilage rides up behind it and assists in shutting off the air passage to block food entering.

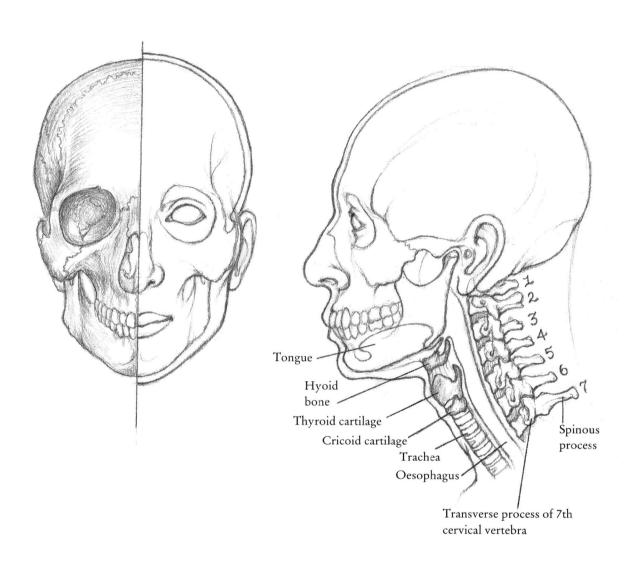

Tongue

Hyoid bone

Thyroid cartilage

Cricoid cartilage

Trachea

Oesophagus

Spinous process

Transverse process of 7th cervical vertebra

1
2
3
4
5
6
7

The mandibular joint (jaw joint)

The jaw joint is a synovial type of joint which is discussed more fully later. The convex head (condyle) of the jaw fits against a concavo-convex area of the skull to make this joint. This is just in front of the external auditory meatus, the opening into the bony canal of the ear. By feeling on yourself where this jaw joint is in relationship to this opening, the placing of the ear can be established.

Both surfaces of bone which are meeting to create the joint are covered by cartilage which is a thin gristly layer of very firm consistency, with a smooth surface. It is a living substance but has no blood or nerve supply, gaining its nutrients from the synovial fluid which fills the joint space.

The jaw joint has a unique disc of cartilage which divides the joint space into upper and lower compartments. This allows a special gliding movement so the head can shift forward in the joint. At this stage a convex surface is meeting another convex surface (when the jaw is depressed and the mouth open) and the round form of the head can be seen in front of the ear, on the surface. Also, when the jaw is moved sideways, the form of the head can be seen and felt on the opposite side to which the jaw is swinging.

By placing the fingers over the joint area, and the thumbs on the angles of the jaw, the heads can be felt, and you will understand better what to look for, in these actions.

Actions of the mandible

The mandible (jaw) is
the only movable bone
of the skull

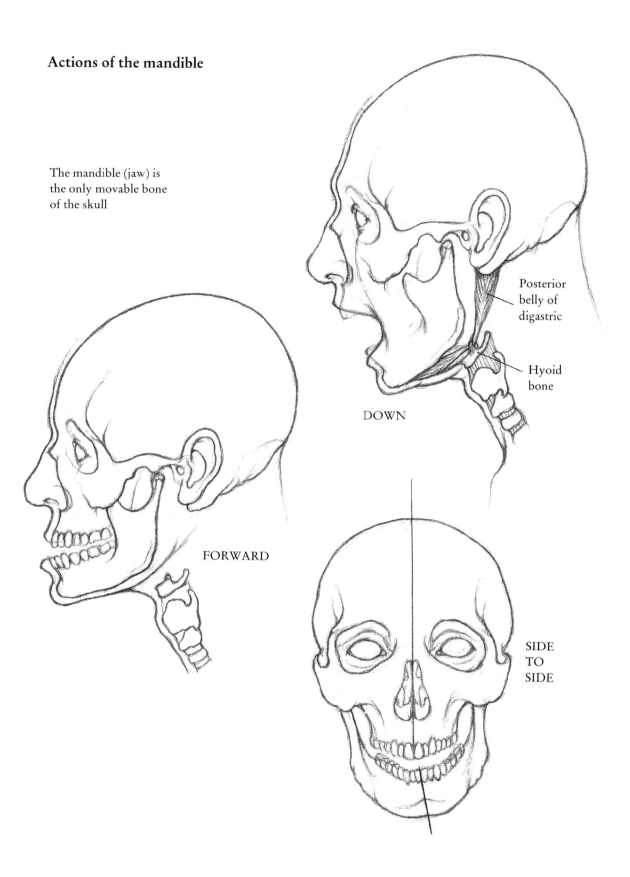

Posterior
belly of
digastric

Hyoid
bone

DOWN

FORWARD

SIDE
TO
SIDE

Muscles controlling the action of the jaw

The TEMPORALIS is fan-shaped, its fleshy part attaching to the temporal bone on the side of the skull, and its tendon passing under the zygomatic arch to insert into the coronoid process of the jaw. When it contracts it works with the contraction of the muscle bundles of the MASSETER, pulling the lower jaw up against the upper jaw, with force, as when the teeth are clenched.

The MASSETER (meaning chewer) is a thick quadrangular muscle. It passes diagonally down and back from its attachment to the zygomatic arch at its lower edge, to the lower border of the ramus of the jaw. It is used in chewing along with four deep muscles. The masseter also protrudes the jaw. This muscle has a rich form on the side of the jaw. By putting the fingers against this area and clenching and unclenching the jaw, the contractions and change of form can be felt. The front border of it is often visible, even though it lies beneath the facial muscles.

The pair of GENIOHYOIDS extend from small tubercles on the inner rim of the chin area of the jaw to the upper part of the body of the hyoid bone. They pull the jaw down closer to the hyoid bone, as the jaw is freer to move.

The pair of MYLOHYOIDS fill the whole triangle under the jaw. Their muscle bundles run downward and medially to intersect in a midline raphe (seam). They also attach to the upper edge of the hyoid bone, and lie in front of the geniohyoids.

The pair of DIGASTRICS each have two bellies joined by a central tendon. The posterior bellies arise from under the mastoid process of the skull. The tendon joining the two bellies is held down to the hyoid bone by a sling of fascia (fibrous tissue). The anterior bellies are attached to the inner rim of the chin area of the jaw. They lie in front of the mylohyoids.

These three muscles constitute the form seen under the chin region. When the neck is stretched backward, there is often a midline indentation caused by the space between the two digastric anterior bellies and the raphe underneath.

These three pairs of muscles act on the hyoid bone to raise and steady it during the act of swallowing. The geniohyoids with the DIGRASTRICS depress the jaw by pulling down on the front margin.

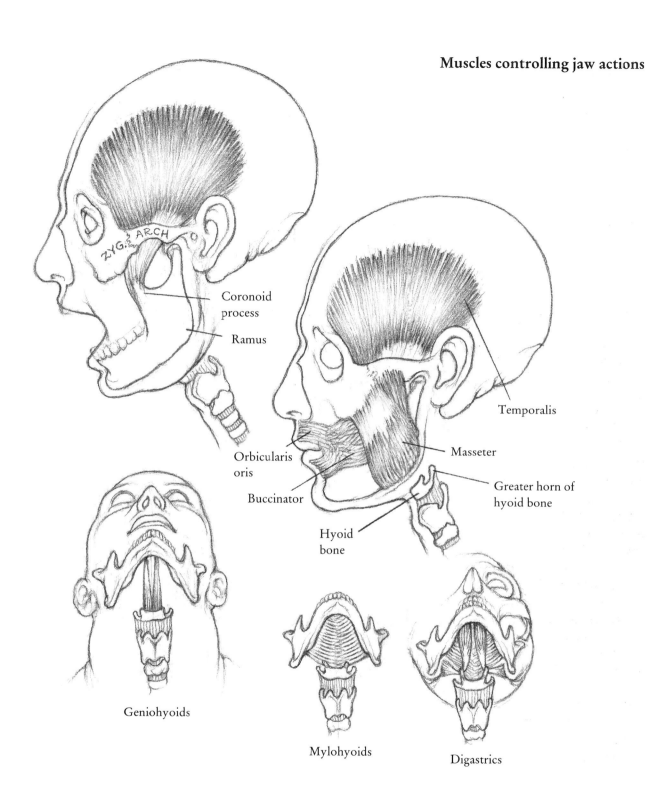

Coronoid process

Ramus

Temporalis

Masseter

Greater horn of hyoid bone

Orbicularis oris

Buccinator

Hyoid bone

Geniohyoids

Mylohyoids

Digastrics

Landmarks of the neck

The internal jugular vein, the internal and external carotid arteries, the sympathetic nerve trunk, and cranial nerves ten, eleven, twelve lie in the anterior triangle, passing deep to the posterior belly of the digastric.

Running diagonally upward, in the posterior triangle, are the three SCALENE muscles, the LEVATOR SCAPULAE above them, and then the SPLENIUS. The scalenes which are attached to the transverse processes of the cervical vertebrae bend the neck to the side when they contract. They are attached to the first and second ribs as shown. The splenius bends the neck and rotates the head to the same side, as it has both cervical vertebrae and skull attachments.

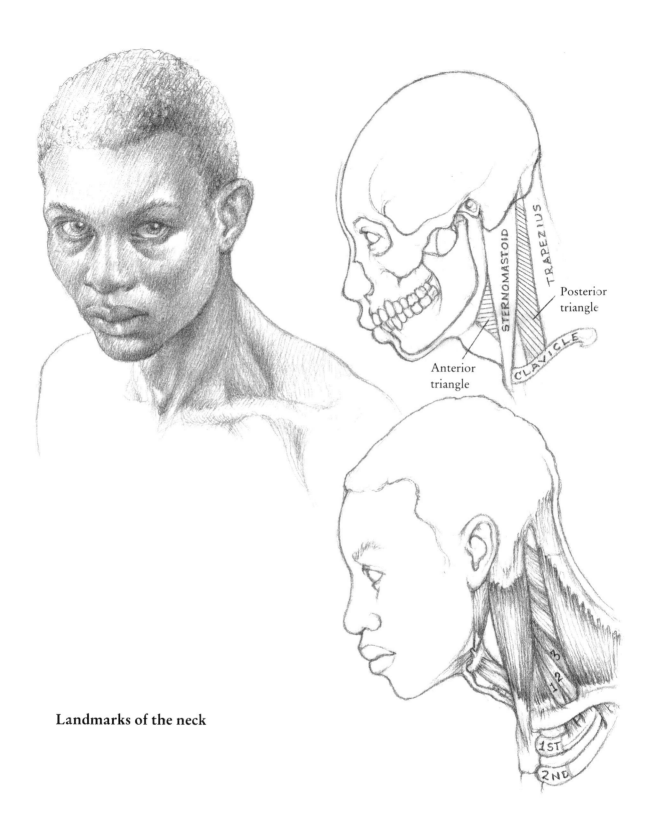

Landmarks of the neck

STERNOMASTOID

TRAPEZIUS

Posterior triangle

CLAVICLE

Anterior triangle

3

2

1

1ST

2ND

The STERNOMASTOID is the most important muscle landmark in the front and side of the neck as its form is always visible. It arises by two attachments, from the sternum and the clavicle. These are called the heads of the sternomastoid. The tendon of the sternal attachment is seen as a taut band as it arises from the front and upper border of the manubrium. The clavicular head is a wide flat tendon and its lateral edge can usually be seen.

The two heads blend together to join a thick form of muscle bundles to make a heavy strap. This strap becomes flatter as it turns upward and back to insert into the mastoid process and also the superior nuchal line at the back of the skull. Remember this is a thick muscle which can catch light and turn away into shadow. It is tempting to delineate it by lines on either side which can deny its form.

Its action, when its cells contract, is to bring the region of its insertion into the mastoid process and the back of the skull closer to the sternum. This is possible because the cervical vertebrae can bend forward or backward, and the head is brought closer to the more immobile sternal area. The sternomastoids are the most obvious, and their contractions can be felt the most when the head is being raised from the pillow.

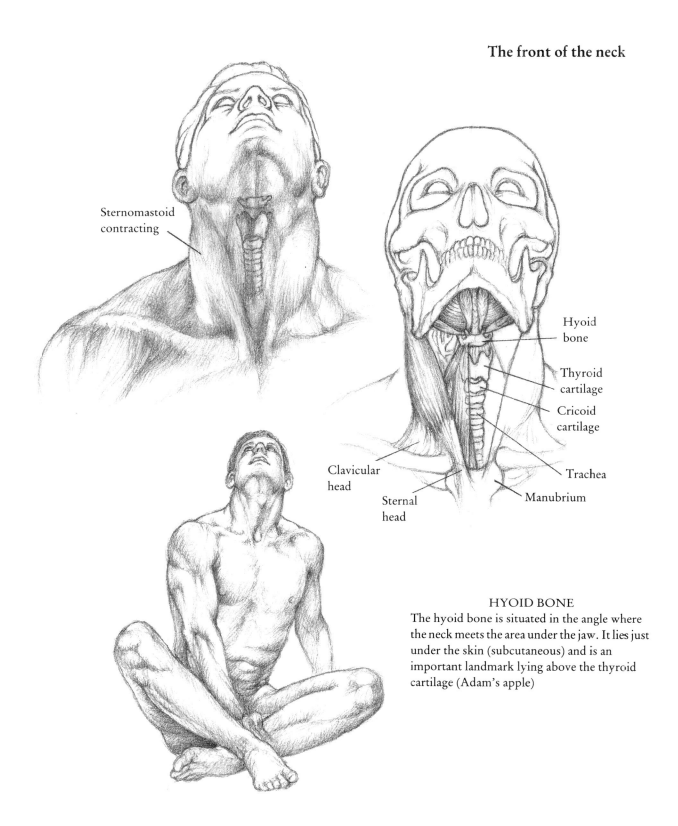

Sternomastoid
contracting

Hyoid
bone

Thyroid
cartilage

Cricoid
cartilage

Clavicular
head

Sternal
head

Trachea

Manubrium

HYOID BONE
The hyoid bone is situated in the angle where
the neck meets the area under the jaw. It lies just
under the skin (subcutaneous) and is an
important landmark lying above the thyroid
cartilage (Adam's apple)

The sternum and the suprasternal notch

The STERNUM (the breast bone) has three parts: the manubrium, the body, and the xiphoid process. The manubrium is the large upper part with a thickened upper border. The sternal ends of the clavicles articulate with it making the sterno-clavicular joints, and altogether they create the suprasternal notch. This is a very important landmark at the root of the neck. Along with the two taut tendons of the sternomastoid arising from the manubrium it is a very valuable area for the artist to look at and palpate.

The body of the sternum is composed of four parts which fuse during development. Sometimes there are apparent ridges where this fusion has taken place. The whole body is joined to the manubrium by a movable joint which acts as a hinge. It allows the body of the sternum, along with the ribs attached to it, to swing up when one breathes in. This can be seen on some people and is called the sternal angle of Louis.

The xiphoid process is ossified in the adult and is a small irregular pointed process sometimes seen.

The whole sternum protects the great vessels of the heart and the heart itself. The upper ten ribs attach to it by their cartilaginous parts which makes a firm but flexible unit to allow for the movement of the rib cage, in breathing.

The suprasternal notch is a stable point to use in taking relative measurements. By using a midline through the sternum and the notch, the angle of the neck and head can be judged. In the position of the female head shown opposite, taking the midpoint of the sternal notch as the anchor point, the distance to her right shoulder edge is approximately the same as to the top of her upper lip.

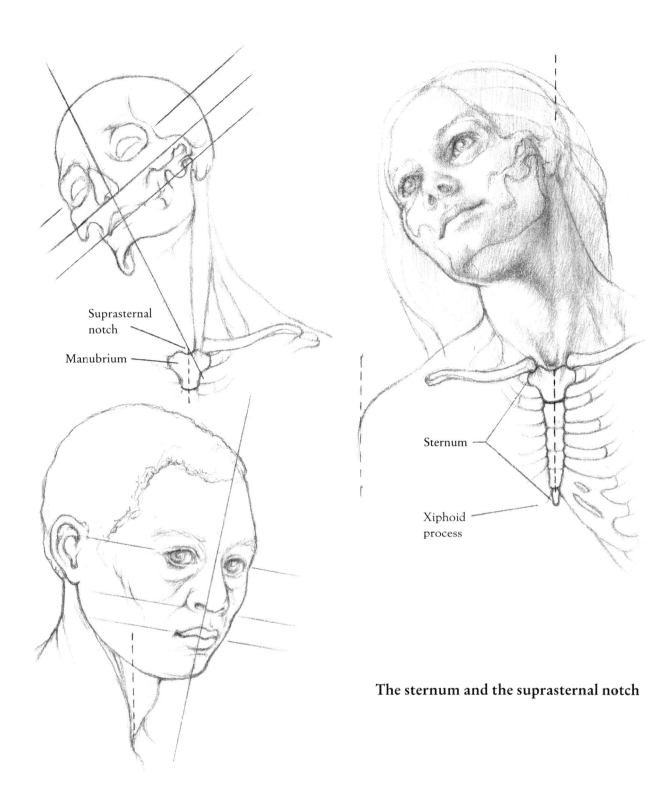

Suprasternal
notch

Manubrium

Sternum

Xiphoid
process

The sternum and the suprasternal notch

27

The neck and the cervical vertebrae

The foramen magnum is a large hole in the inferior surface of the skull through which the brain is continuous with the spinal cord. On either side of this foramen are paired lumps of bone shaped like rockers with smooth elliptical surfaces which are convex. These two convex surfaces articulate with two concave elliptical surfaces on the superior surface of the first vertebra, the ATLAS. The action possible because of this design is to allow the head to 'rock' on the neck in the nodding action to give the 'yes' answer. The paired lumps of bone on the skull are called the occipital condyles.

The second cervical vertebra is called the AXIS. From its vertebral body there is a peg of bone called the dens, which projects upward to lie against the atlas and articulate with it. It is held there by a ligament. This dens allows the atlas to pivot, and thus create the 'no' answer. These are important and unique actions of the head in its relationship with the neck.

The LIGAMENTUM NUCHAE is the continuation in the neck of the fibrous ligaments which tie the vertebrae together. It is a strong thin sheet in the midline at the back of the neck, attaching to the skull and the spines of the seven cervical vertebrae. Two muscles, the splenius and the trapezius are attached to it. A linear indentation is often seen in the midline running up the back of the neck. It is caused by the muscles pulling on the edge of the ligamentum nuchae, the muscles contracting and mounding up on either side of it.

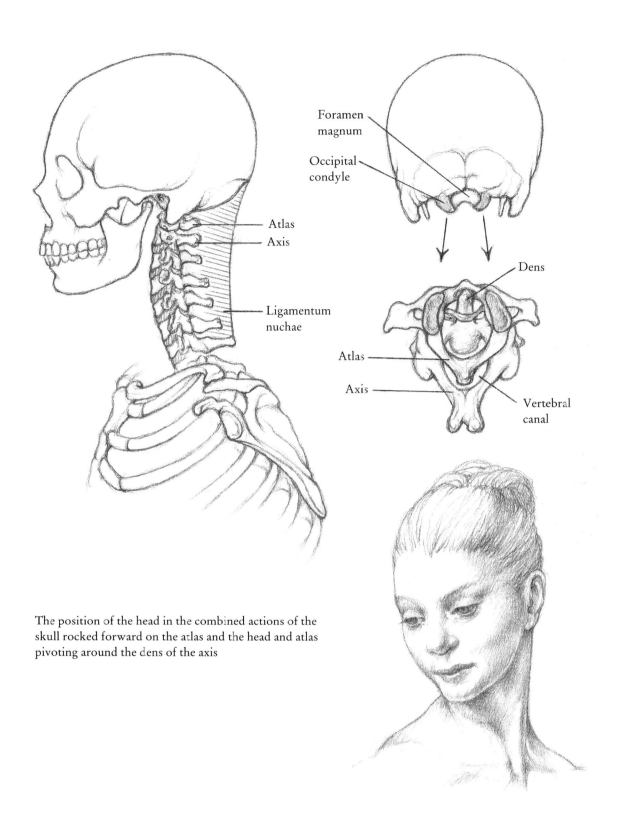

Foramen
magnum

Occipital
condyle

Atlas
Axis

Ligamentum
nuchae

Dens

Atlas

Axis

Vertebral
canal

The position of the head in the combined actions of the
skull rocked forward on the atlas and the head and atlas
pivoting around the dens of the axis

The general actions of the cervical part of the vertebral column are that it can bend in all directions and can rotate also, with limitations. The articular discs between the vertebrae, which allow action, are generous.

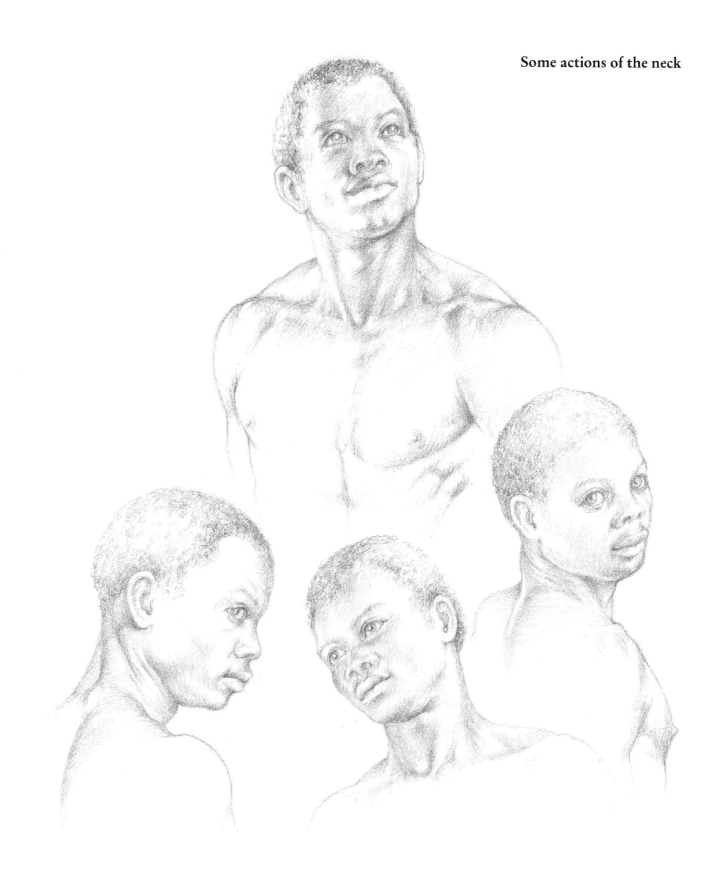

The pectoral girdle

The PECTORAL GIRDLE consists of two bones, the clavicle and the scapula. The clavicle is S-shaped, convex forward in its rounded medial two-thirds, and concave forward in its remaining third, which is flattened. The medial end is enlarged and makes a joint with the manubrium called the sterno-clavicular joint. The lateral end makes a joint with the acromion process of the scapula. The acromion is the large flat free end of the spine of the scapula, which projects out to the point of the shoulder.

The form of the clavicle with its rounded and flattened parts can usually be seen as the clavicle lies just under the skin (subcutaneous). Its enlarged head making its joint with the manubrium is also a landmark. On the top of the shoulder both the end of the clavicle and the flattened surface of the acromion have visible forms as they are subcutaneous.

In the drawing, the humerus is included with its head making a joint with the articular shallow cup, the glenoid fossa, of the scapula. When the arm is raised the scapula rotates. Its lower point, the inferior angle, swings forward and up around the rib cage. The glenoid fossa with the head of the humerus rise, and the acromion and lateral end of the clavicle also.

The clavicle and the acromion can be palpated readily on yourself, while they are at rest, and during movment, and their forms studied on yourself in a mirror.

**The neck
and
the pectoral girdle**

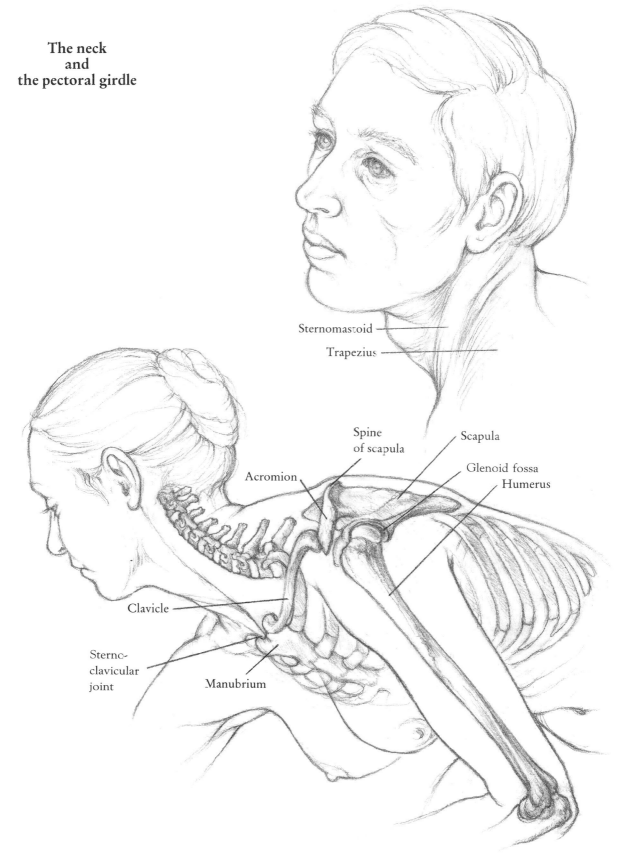

Sternomastoid

Trapezius

Spine
of scapula

Scapula

Acromion

Glenoid fossa

Humerus

Clavicle

Sterno-
clavicular
joint

Manubrium

Joints

Action takes place in a body because the bones of the skeleton make joints (articulate) with each other, and because muscles act on these joints.

There are three main classes of joints: FIBROUS, CARTILAGINOUS and SYNOVIAL.

FIBROUS joints are those in which two bones are joined together by fibrous tissue which is composed of strands of non-living material with cells interspersed and, at times, elastic fibres. This plan exists where movement is not desired but a little flexibility may be needed.

CARTILAGINOUS joints exist between the vertebrae of the vertebral column. Here a pliable fibro-cartilaginous cushion is present called a vertebral disc. It is a shock absorber, and it is covered by a capsule of layers of diagonal fibres. This allows the vertebrae to 'squeeze down' a little on the softer disc so the vertebral column can bend. The diagonal fibres of the capsule which are attached to the vertebrae above and below the disc strengthen the joint and also allow for rotation.

SYNOVIAL joints are those in which the articulating ends of two bones are contained within a capsule which contains synovial lubricating fluid. The main joints of the body which allow greater movement are of this class. They include the shoulder joint (ball and socket), the hip joint (ball and socket), the elbow joint (hinge and pivotal), the knee joint (hinge) which is considered here, and others.

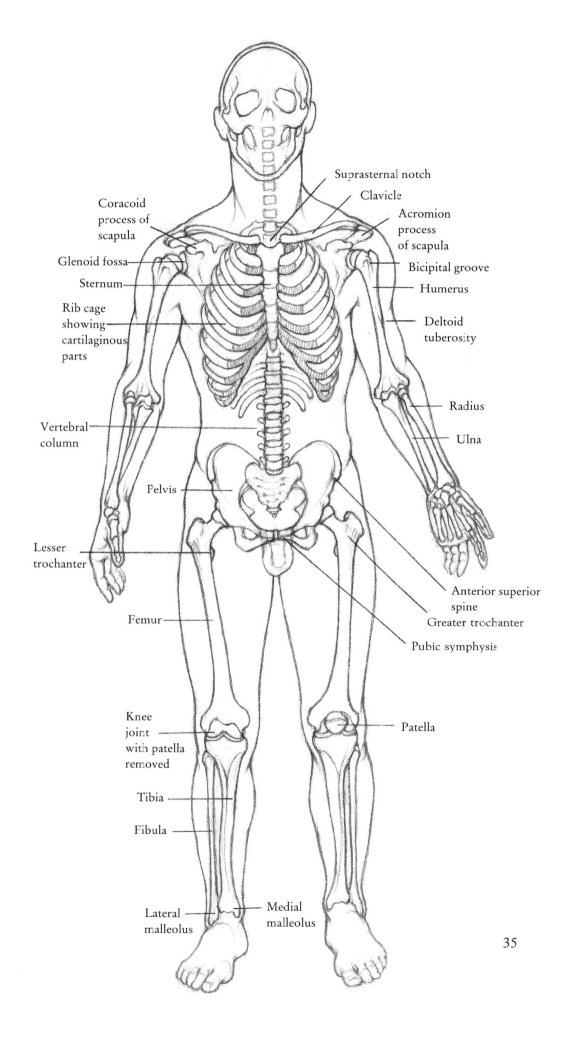

Coracoid process of scapula

Glenoid fossa

Sternum

Rib cage showing cartilaginous parts

Vertebral column

Pelvis

Lesser trochanter

Femur

Knee joint with patella removed

Tibia

Fibula

Lateral malleolus

Suprasternal notch

Clavicle

Acromion process of scapula

Bicipital groove

Humerus

Deltoid tuberosity

Radius

Ulna

Anterior superior spine

Greater trochanter

Pubic symphysis

Patella

Medial malleolus

35

The synovial joint of the knee

The knee joint is chosen as an example of synovial joint structure because the landmarks are very visible and it is a most important region in figure work. A simple synovial joint is discussed first.

A simple synovial joint (as those between the three bones in each of the fingers) has a convex surface on one bone fitting against a concave surface on a second bone. The bone ends are covered by a thin layer of articular cartilage. The cartilage which has no blood or nerve supply is kept alive by the synovial fluid which fills the joint space. This fluid is produced by the synovial membrane which lines the capsule of the joint. The whole joint is enclosed by a capsule of fibrous tissue, and in many cases ligaments composed of fibrous tissue and some elastic fibres form also to join the bones together to add strength and guard against bone displacement. For the artists this means that at joint areas there are the specialized enlarged ends of bones to consider in the form as well as the build up of the soft tissue.

In the knee joint, the lower end of the femur has two convex surfaces called the medial and lateral condyles. They are convex front to back as well as side to side, a rocker shape. They fit against two shallow surfaces on the top of the tibia which are called the tibial medial and lateral condyles. These condyles are all covered by a layer of cartilage. On the upper surface of the tibia are semilunar cartilages around the rims of the condyles and part of the surfaces which create an extra cushion for absorbing weight and shock. These are a factor also in controlling movement of the femoral condyles sideways. Two ligaments, the cruciate ligaments, join the bones together within the joint space.

At the front of the joint is the patella, a sesamoid bone (seed) which has developed within the tendon of the QUADRICEPS (four heads) FEMORIS. It is the only muscle on the front of the thigh. The posterior part of the patella is wedge-shaped to fit between the condyles. As the knee bends and straightens the patella is accommodated in the furrow. The tendon of the quadriceps femoris inserts into the tibial tuberosity, a large V-shaped mass of bone on the front of the tibia. The part of the tendon from the lower edge of the patella to the tuberosity is called the patellar tendon. Like all tendons it remains approximately the same length during knee action.

SCHEME OF SIMPLE SYNOVIAL JOINT

SCHEME OF STRUCTURES OF THE KNEE JOINT (LATERAL ASPECT)

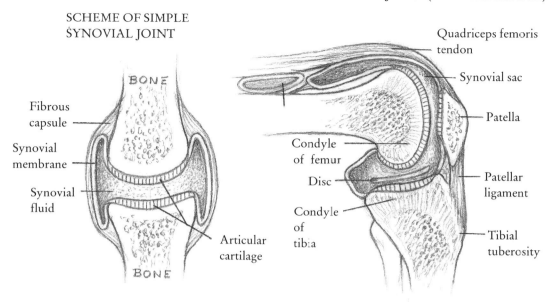

Fibrous capsule

Synovial membrane

Synovial fluid

BONE

BONE

Articular cartilage

Quadriceps femoris tendon

Synovial sac

Patella

Condyle of femur

Disc

Condyle of tibia

Patellar ligament

Tibial tuberosity

THE LEFT KNEE JOINT IN THE SITTING POSITION (ANTERIOR ASPECT)

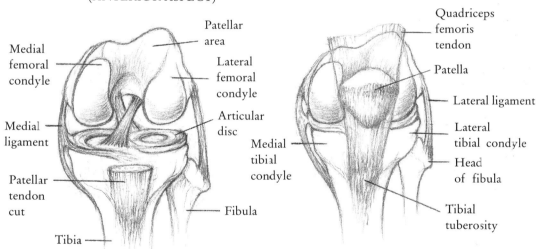

Medial femoral condyle

Medial ligament

Patellar tendon cut

Tibia

Patellar area

Lateral femoral condyle

Articular disc

Fibula

Quadriceps femoris tendon

Patella

Lateral ligament

Lateral tibial condyle

Head of fibula

Tibial tuberosity

Medial tibial condyle

The femur and tibia are pulled apart to show structures, and the patella is removed

QUADRICEPS FEMORIS is the only muscle on the front of the thigh and the only one which can extend the leg. When its fleshy parts shorten they pull on the tendon which is inserting into the tibial tuberosity, and pull the tibia in alignment with the femur. Quadriceps is composed of four muscles which have a common insertion.

VASTUS INTERMEDIUS lies deep and is attached to the front of the femur. RECTUS FEMORIS spans the hip joint and has its origin from the anterior inferior spine of the pelvis and the rim of the socket for the head of the femur. The socket is called the acetabulum. The muscle bundles are short and bipennate in design. When they shorten they create a bulging form on the front of the thigh. The precise flat shape of the tendon above the patella can usually be seen.

VASTUS MEDIALIS and VASTUS LATERALIS arise from the back of the femur along the linea aspera. They surround the femur as they wrap around it, medially and laterally, to insert into the patella at the front. The forms of these two muscles are very apparent on the inside and outside of the leg. The medialis inserts into two-thirds of the medial border of the patella and also a small part of its base (the upper border). The lateralis inserts into the rest of the base and a little of its lateral side.

This muscle is greatly developed in ballet dancers, and in athletes who use their legs in the extended action as in walking and kicking.

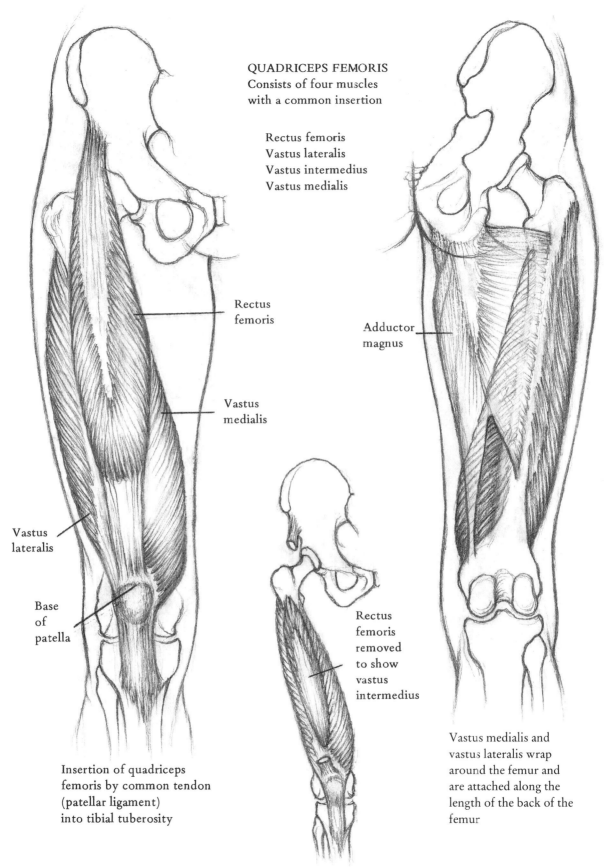

QUADRICEPS FEMORIS
Consists of four muscles
with a common insertion

Rectus femoris
Vastus lateralis
Vastus intermedius
Vastus medialis

Rectus
femoris

Vastus
medialis

Adductor
magnus

Vastus
lateralis

Base
of
patella

Rectus
femoris
removed
to show
vastus
intermedius

Insertion of quadriceps
femoris by common tendon
(patellar ligament)
into tibial tuberosity

Vastus medialis and
vastus lateralis wrap
around the femur and
are attached along the
length of the back of the
femur

The vertebral column and the vertebrae

The vertebral column is the central axis of the back of the trunk. The column has five regions: seven cervical vertebrae, twelve thoracic vertebrae, five lumbar vertebrae, the sacrum and the coccyx. Except for the first two cervical vertebrae, the cervical, thoracic and lumbar all have cushions between them of fibro-gelatinous substance called the nucleus pulposus. This is surrounded by a tough fibrous capsule which binds the two vertebrae together. These are called articular discs and act as shock absorbers as well as allowing for action between the vertebrae. The fibres of the capsule are arranged in layers, and they run diagonally to each other. This gives both strength and mobility to the joint. Each vertebrae is weight supporting and the vertebrae increase in size down to the fifth lumbar. At this point weight is transferred to the sacrum and then out to the two hip bones. From that point it is transferred to the legs if one is standing or to the two ischial tuberosities of the pelvis on which one sits.

Each vertebrae is different to some degree but there is a common patterning. The weight bearing part is called the body and consists of a small cylindrical block of bone greater in width than in height. It is covered on its upper and lower surfaces with cartilage. From the back of this solid cylinder an arch of bone projects which creates a hole. When the vertebrae are placed on top of each other these holes create a continous canal, the vertebral canal, in which the spinal cord is enclosed. Where each vertebra meets the next vertebra a small area of the spinal cord is exposed at the intervertebral foramen, and it is through this foramen that each segmental nerve emerges to supply its segment of the body. A transverse process of bone projects from either side of the arch, and a spinous process from the back. These serve as levers for muscle attachments, and these muscles by contracting cause the column to bend and also rotate in actions required by the body.

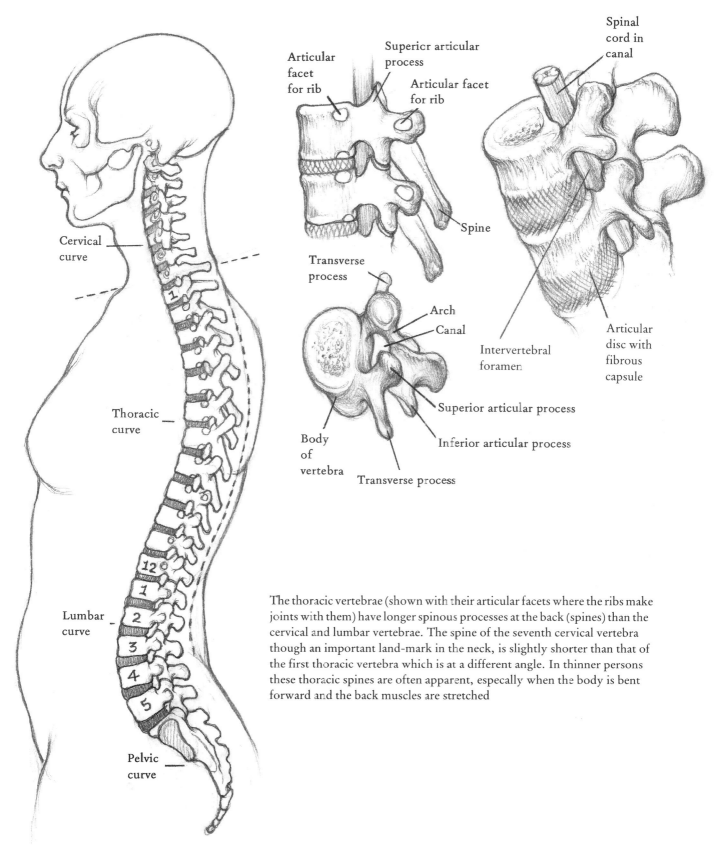

Cervical curve

Thoracic curve

Lumbar curve

Pelvic curve

Articular facet for rib

Superior articular process

Articular facet for rib

Spine

Spinal cord in canal

Transverse process

Arch

Canal

Intervertebral foramen

Articular disc with fibrous capsule

Body of vertebra

Superior articular process

Inferior articular process

Transverse process

The thoracic vertebrae (shown with their articular facets where the ribs make joints with them) have longer spinous processes at the back (spines) than the cervical and lumbar vertebrae. The spine of the seventh cervical vertebra though an important land-mark in the neck, is slightly shorter than that of the first thoracic vertebra which is at a different angle. In thinner persons these thoracic spines are often apparent, especially when the body is bent forward and the back muscles are stretched

The curves of the vertebral column

The vertebral column has four curves which give the basic rhythm to the body. The cervical curve is composed of seven vertebrae and their discs. It begins to develop late in uterine life and begins to become convex forward when the child begins to hold up its head. The thoracic curve is concave forward, is composed of twelve vertebrae and is present at birth. The lumbar curve is convex forward and appears when the child begins to walk at about eighteen months. It becomes more prominent in the female than in the male because the fifth lumbar vertebra articulates with the sacrum of the pelvis which has a more forward tilt in the female. This creates a more backward thrust of the buttocks. The pelvic curve, concave forward, is composed of five sacral vertebrae and the coccyx which has four vestigial tail vertebrae. The sacral vertebrae are fused in the adult and create the flat area seen just below the prominent lumbar curve.

43

Actions of the vertebral column

There is greater action possible in both bending and rotation in the cervical and lumbar areas of the vertebral column than in the thoracic area. This is because the cervical and lumbar vertebrae have more generous articular discs between them. Also, the thoracic vertebrae are limited in action by the joints which the ribs have with them, and the very strong fibres at each joint.

In the male figure, the two muscle straps of the rectus abdominis which are attached to the front of the rib cage and to the front of the pubis, by contracting, bring these two areas closer together.

In the female figure, the sacrospinales which is attached the whole length of the back from skull to pelvis, by contracting, bring the skull and the pelvis closer together.

Lumbar

Thoracic

Cervical

Muscles of the anterior aspect of the body

The PECTORALIS MAJOR is a large fan-shaped muscle on the chest wall. It has two parts, or heads as they are called, originating from the clavicle and the rib cage. The clavicular head is attached to one half of the anterior (front) and medial (towards the midline) part of the clavicle. The sternal head attaches to the area of the sterno-clavicular joint, the sternum, and the fifth and sixth costal cartilages. The muscle is inserted into the top part of the humerus. When the pectoralis contracts, the humerus being freer to move than the thorax, changes position. The insertion has a special feature as the lower muscle bundles of the sternal head roll under as they pass from the chest to the humerus, in one twist. This plan provides more mobility for the humerus.

When the arm is relaxed, this whole rolled border can be grasped in the hand. It creates the front 'wing' of the arm pit and is a form which can always be seen. When the arm is brought forward against resistance the two heads are often seen as separate entities. The main action it provides is adducting (bringing toward the midline) the arm.

The BICEPS (meaning two heads) has two tendinous origins. The long head is attached to the scapula just above the glenoid fossa and the short head is attached to the coracoid process. The long head lies in a special groove in the bone at the top end of the humerus. It is held in that bicipital groove by a fibrous ligament which creates a tunnel for it. The long and short heads meet to form the belly of the biceps, and the insertion of the muscle is into the tuberosity of the radius. The biceps flexes (bends toward the body) the elbow joint, and is also the powerful supinator of the forearm. Because the radius can rotate in its socket, when the biceps contracts, the radius is pulled over the ulna and the forearm and hand are turned over.

The tendon of the pectoralis passes on top of the biceps to its attachment on the far edge (the lateral lip) of the bicipital groove.

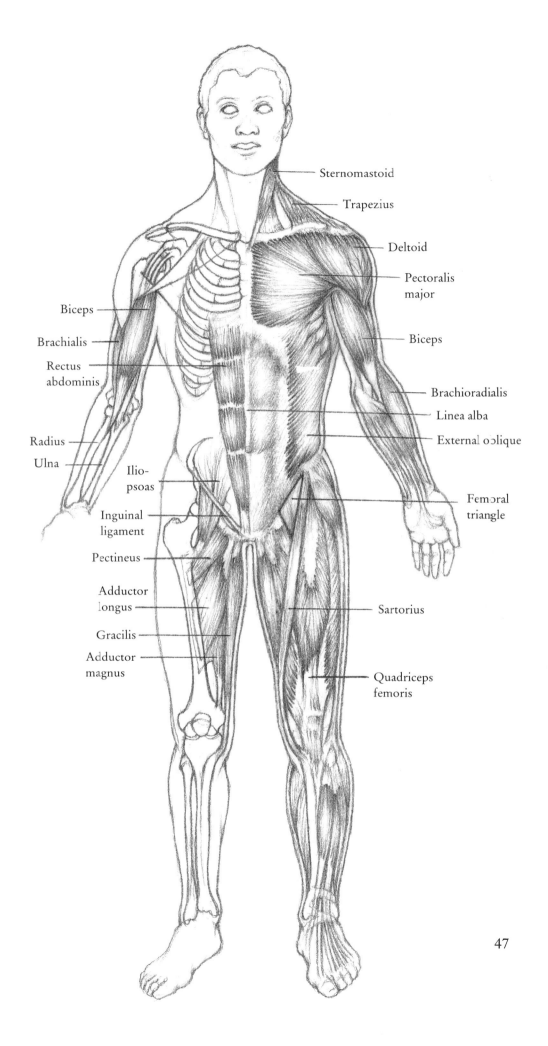

Sternomastoid

Trapezius

Deltoid

Pectoralis
major

Biceps

Biceps

Brachialis

Rectus
abdominis

Brachioradialis

Linea alba

External oblique

Radius

Ulna

Ilio-
psoas

Femoral
triangle

Inguinal
ligament

Pectineus

Adductor
longus

Sartorius

Gracilis

Adductor
magnus

Quadriceps
femoris

The RECTUS ABDOMINIS is composed of two straps attached above to the xiphoid process and the cartilages of the fifth, sixth and seventh ribs. Below it is attached to the front of the pubis. Each strap has an attachment about 76 mm across at the rib cage and about 25 mm across at the pubis. The lateral borders are therefore diagonal. There are fibrous horizontal intersections in the muscle because it is of segmental origin. These are at the level of the xipohoid, the umbilicus, and half way between. The whole muscle is enclosed in a sheath, which are sheets of aponeurotic tissue (flattened tendon) of the waist muscles which are discussed later. Above the umbilicus the pair of straps are separated and the sheath meets in the midline which shows as an indentation on the surface. It is called the linea alba (white line). Below the umbilicus the pair of straps are closer together but an indentation can often be seen here, especially if the muscles are well developed.

When the rectus abdominis contracts it brings the front of the rib cage and the front of the pelvis closer together. It is used to raise the body from the lying position to the sitting position and is a very important muscle. Also, its form is important for the artist.

The SARTORIUS is the longest muscle in the body, a narrow strap, which arises from the anterior superior spine and the bone below and is inserted by a long flattened tendon into the medial surface of the upper part of the shaft of the tibia. When it contracts (by about 15 cm) it flexes the hip joint, rotates the thigh laterally and flexes the knee. When both muscles are working it brings the legs into the cross-legged position a tailor (sartor) used to assume at work. For the artist, although its form may not be seen clearly, there is a definite feel of the muscle as it creates a long diagonal across the front of the thigh dividing the front aspect of the thigh into two forms.

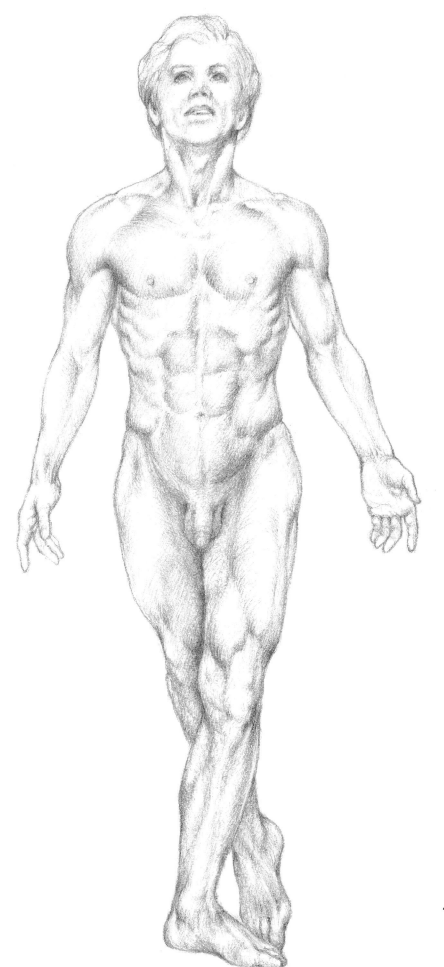

The adductors and flexors of the thigh

The ILIOPSOAS has two parts. One arises from the inner surface of the hip bone and the other from the sides and bodies of the lumbar vertebrae and their discs. It flexes the hip, pulling it up toward the trunk. The muscles pass under the inguinal ligament and attach to the lesser trochanter of the femur. The femoral artery, vein and nerve which supply the front of the thigh lie on the front of this muscle and behind the inguinal ligament. This is a depressed area on the thigh, to be looked for, and is called the femoral triangle.

The PECTINEUS, ADDUCTOR LONGUS, ADDUCTOR BREVIS which lies beneath the longus, and the ADDUCTOR MAGNUS all arise from the front of the pubis. They insert into the femur at the back along the roughened line of bone which they partially create by their pull on it, called the linea aspera.

The word adductor means to bring or lead to the midline. The adductor muscles draw the femur to the midline when they contract and can also draw one thigh over the other. They also flex the thigh by pulling the femur up toward the pelvis.

For the artist all of these muscles are usually seen as one great form on the inner region of the thigh. When they are working, adducting or flexing, the form will thicken and change, in action. The GRACILIS is also included with this group adducting the thigh but as it inserts into the upper part of the medial surface of the tibia, it flexes the knee and not the thigh.

When the leg is thrust away from the body (abduction – to lead away) these muscles can become more delineated as they are then stretched.

The muscles of the abdomen

Three flat muscles form the abdominal wall along with the rectus abdominis. They are arranged in three layers with their muscle bundles running in three different directions, in the region of the waist. This is a strong and flexible arrangement both for movement (rotation and bending) and for binding the rib cage and costal margin to the pelvis. They also help keep the abdominal viscera in place. Their tendons are flattened into a sheet called an aponeurosis, which blend together at the front of the abdomen and then split to pass in front and behind the rectus abdominis muscle to form a sheath for it.

The lateral edges where the sheath is dividing to go to the front and back of the rectus abdominis is an apparent form. And so is the flattened form of the aponeurosis on either side.

The TRANSVERSUS is the innermost layer and its muscle bundles run in a transverse direction. It has its origin from the inguinal ligament, the iliac crest, the transverse processes of the lumbar vertebrae and by fleshy slips from the inner surface of the lower six costal cartilages.

The middle layer the INTERNAL OBLIQUE has its origin from the anterior two-thirds of the iliac crest and from more than half the inguinal ligament. It is inserted into the lower four ribs.

The outermost layer is the EXTERNAL OBLIQUE and has its origin from the lower eight ribs on the antero-lateral aspect of the rib cage. The muscle bundles run downward and medially. These fleshy digitations of origin interlock like fingers with the digitations of the serratus anterior muscle and with those of the latissimus dorsi. The lowest bundles insert by tendinous fibres into the iliac crest between its mid-point and the anterior superior spine. This spine is a very important landmark of the pelvis for the artist to note. In the female it turns slightly outward, in the male it usually turns slightly inward. The rest of the insertion of the external oblique is through the sheet of aponeurosis which covers the abdomen. The lower edge of this sheet is considered 'free' between the anterior superior spine and the pubic tubercle, a small process of bone for muscle attachment on the pubis. The sheet creates a linear tension between these two points, a definite landmark for the artist, and this 'edge' is called the inguinal ligament.

The aponeurosis of the transversus, internal and external oblique muscles contribute to the covering for the scrotum as the testes descend before birth from within the abdomen, pass downward and forward over the pubis and carry the elongated and thinned aponeurosis over it.

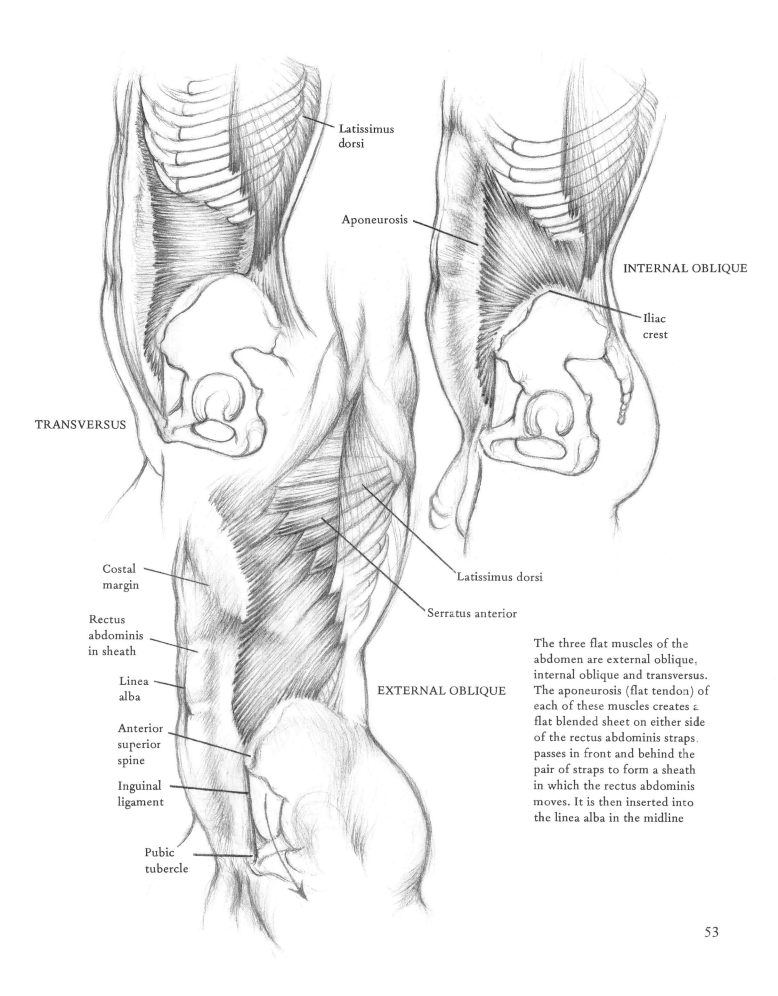

Latissimus
dorsi

Aponeurosis

INTERNAL OBLIQUE

Iliac
crest

TRANSVERSUS

Costal
margin

Rectus
abdominis
in sheath

Linea
alba

Anterior
superior
spine

Inguinal
ligament

Pubic
tubercle

Latissimus dorsi

Serratus anterior

EXTERNAL OBLIQUE

The three flat muscles of the
abdomen are external oblique,
internal oblique and transversus.
The aponeurosis (flat tendon) of
each of these muscles creates a
flat blended sheet on either side
of the rectus abdominis straps,
passes in front and behind the
pair of straps to form a sheath
in which the rectus abdominis
moves. It is then inserted into
the linea alba in the midline

53

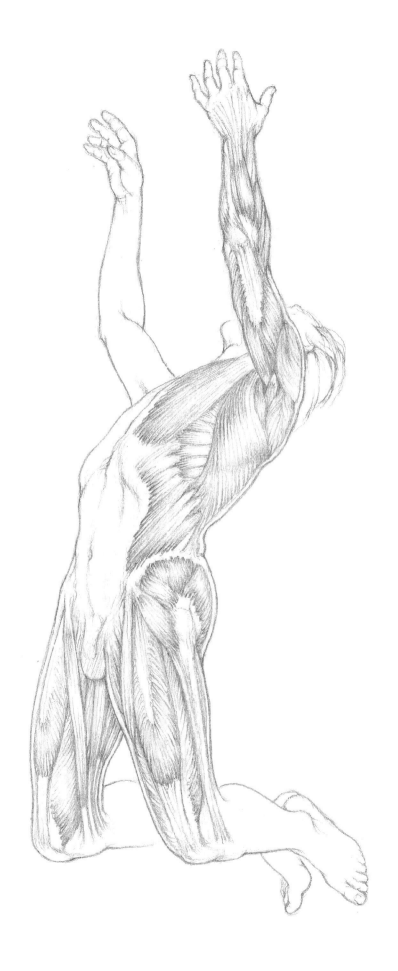

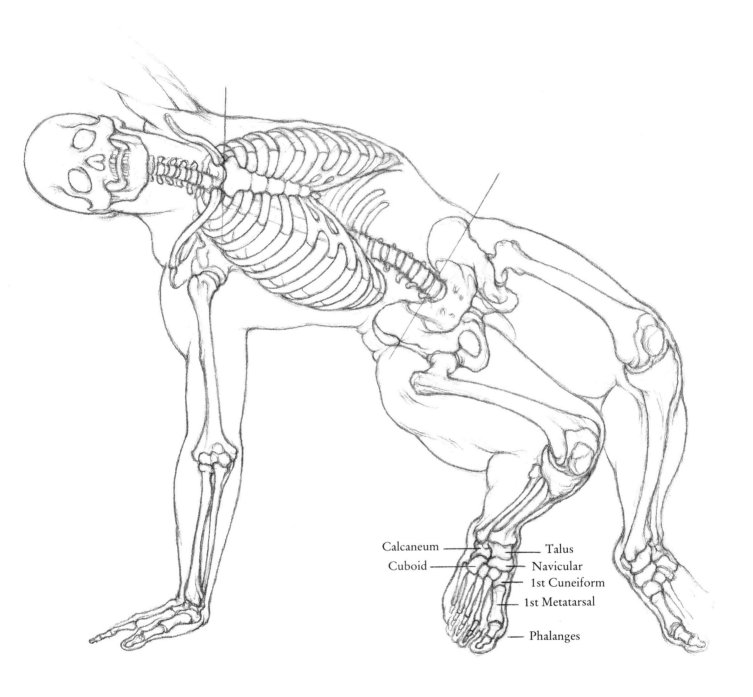

Calcaneum ———

Cuboid ———

——— Talus

——— Navicular

——— 1st Cuneiform

——— 1st Metatarsal

——— Phalanges

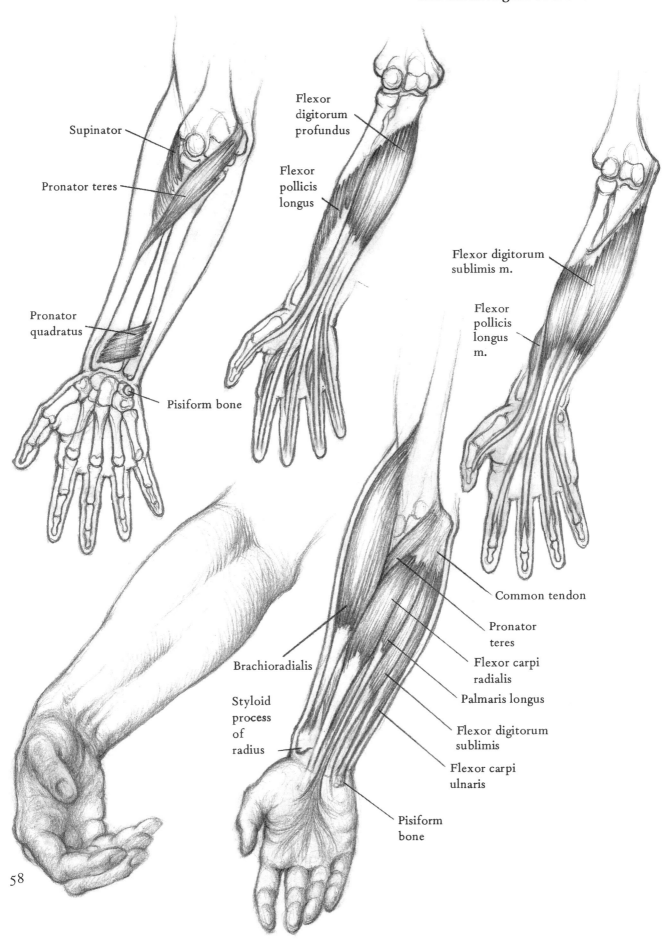

Supinator

Pronator teres

Pronator
quadratus

Pisiform bone

Flexor
digitorum
profundus

Flexor
pollicis
longus

Flexor digitorum
sublimis m.

Flexor
pollicis
longus
m.

Common tendon

Pronator
teres

Flexor carpi
radialis

Palmaris longus

Flexor digitorum
sublimis

Flexor carpi
ulnaris

Brachioradialis

Styloid
process
of
radius

Pisiform
bone

58

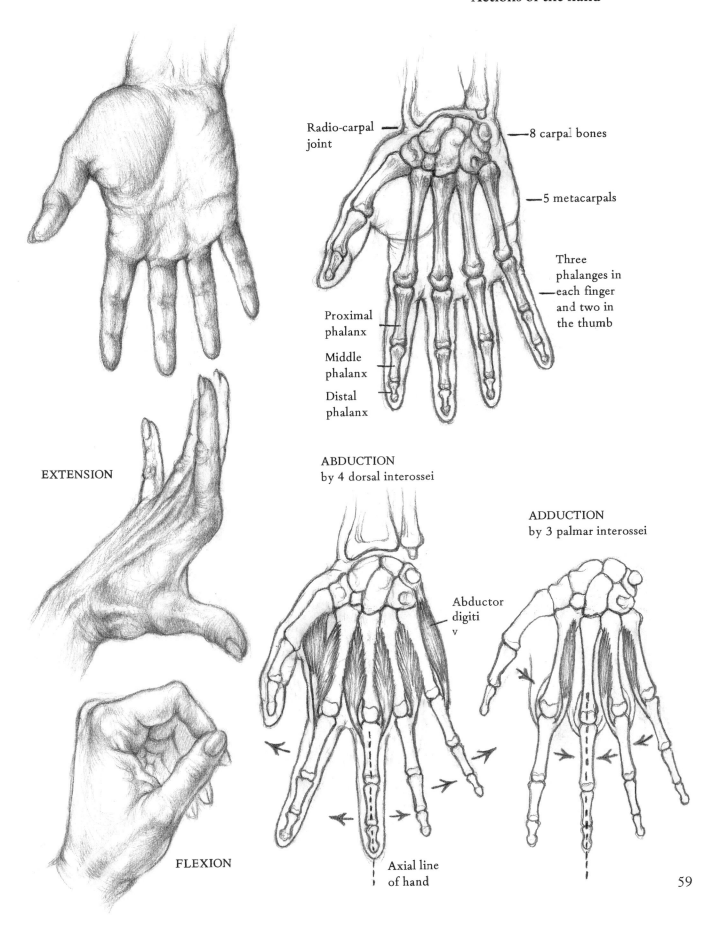

Radio-carpal joint

8 carpal bones

5 metacarpals

Three phalanges in each finger and two in the thumb

Proximal phalanx

Middle phalanx

Distal phalanx

EXTENSION

ABDUCTION
by 4 dorsal interossei

ADDUCTION
by 3 palmar interossei

Abductor digiti v

FLEXION

Axial line of hand

59

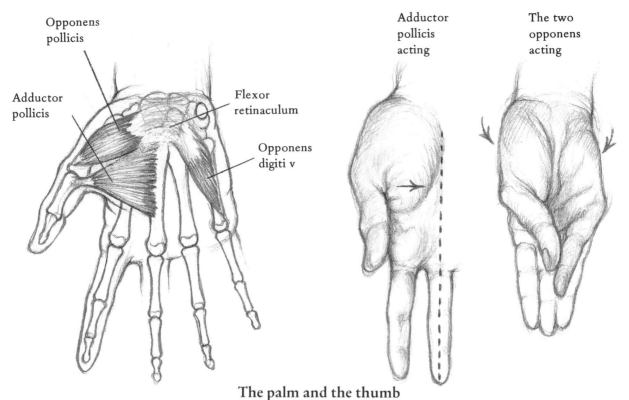

Opponens
pollicis

Adductor
pollicis

Flexor
retinaculum

Opponens
digiti v

Adductor
pollicis
acting

The two
opponens
acting

The palm and the thumb

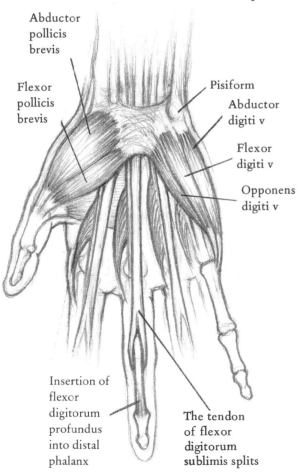

Abductor
pollicis
brevis

Flexor
pollicis
brevis

Pisiform

Abductor
digiti v

Flexor
digiti v

Opponens
digiti v

Insertion of
flexor
digitorum
profundus
into distal
phalanx

The tendon
of flexor
digitorum
sublimis splits

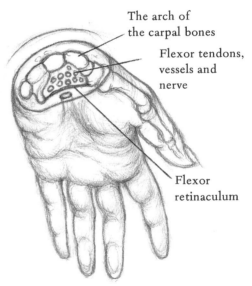

The arch of
the carpal bones

Flexor tendons,
vessels and
nerve

Flexor
retinaculum

The carpal bones form
an arch at the wrist
under which the flexor
tendons lie protected.
A fibrous ligament called
the flexor retinaculum
spans these, attaches
to the medial and lateral
carpals, and maintains
the arch

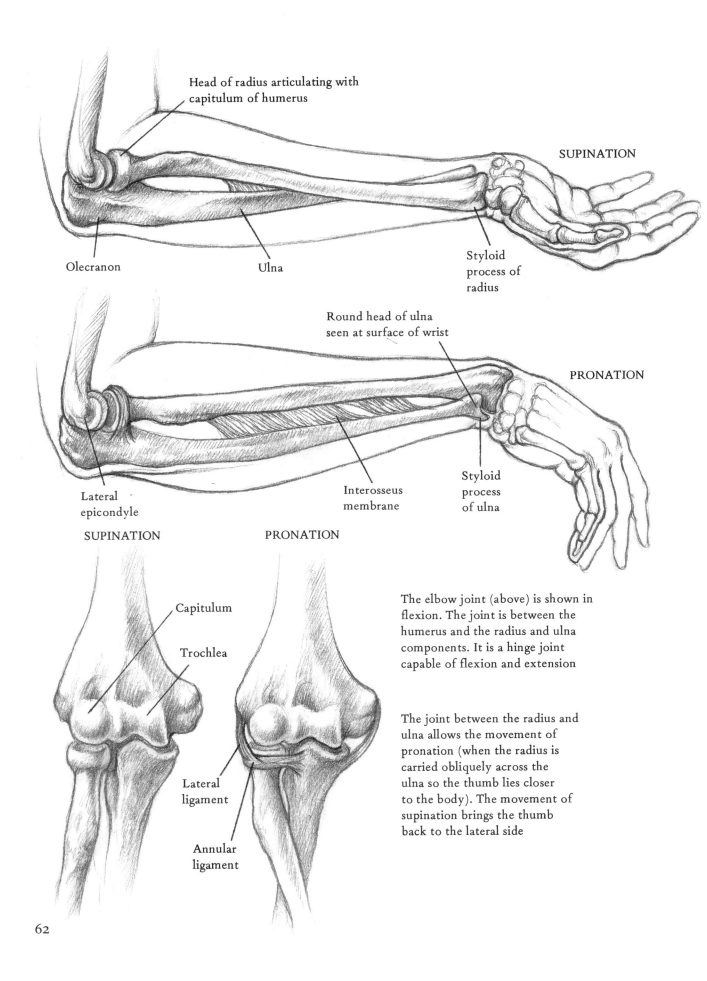

Head of radius articulating with capitulum of humerus

SUPINATION

Olecranon

Ulna

Styloid process of radius

Round head of ulna seen at surface of wrist

PRONATION

Lateral epicondyle

Interosseus membrane

Styloid process of ulna

SUPINATION   PRONATION

Capitulum

Trochlea

Lateral ligament

Annular ligament

The elbow joint (above) is shown in flexion. The joint is between the humerus and the radius and ulna components. It is a hinge joint capable of flexion and extension

The joint between the radius and ulna allows the movement of pronation (when the radius is carried obliquely across the ulna so the thumb lies closer to the body). The movement of supination brings the thumb back to the lateral side

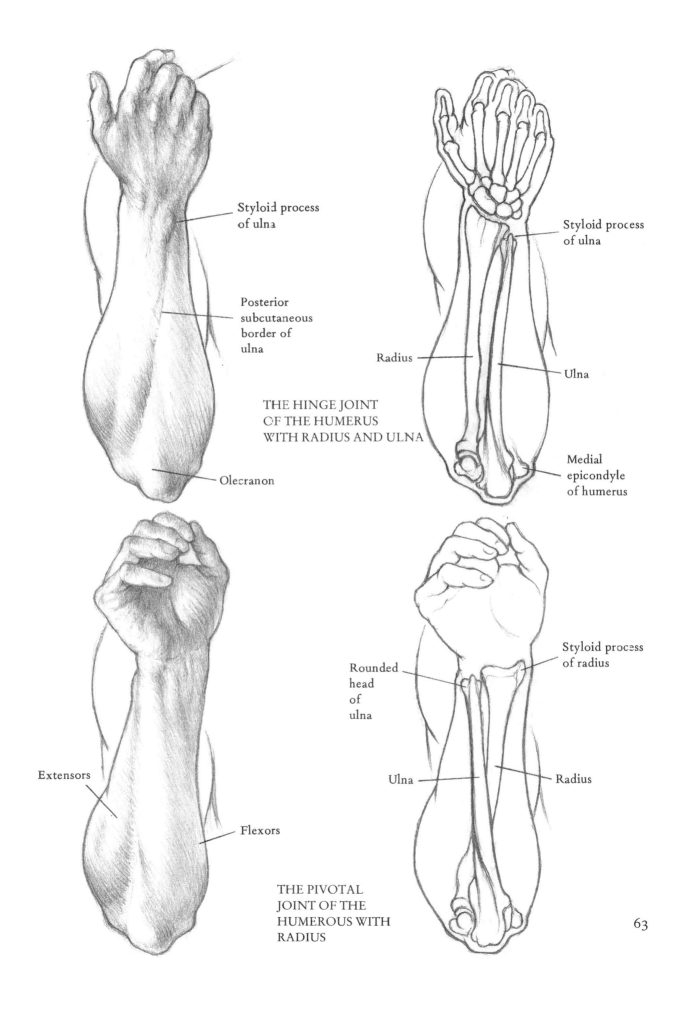

Styloid process
of ulna

Posterior
subcutaneous
border of
ulna

Olecranon

Styloid process
of ulna

Radius

Ulna

THE HINGE JOINT
OF THE HUMERUS
WITH RADIUS AND ULNA

Medial
epicondyle
of humerus

Extensors

Flexors

Rounded
head
of
ulna

Styloid process
of radius

Ulna

Radius

THE PIVOTAL
JOINT OF THE
HUMEROUS WITH
RADIUS

63

The areas of the shoulder and arms are accented to show the main muscles which are working to produce this section.

The deltoid has three parts. The anterior part is attached to the clavicle, the middle part is attached to the edge of the acromion and the posterior part to the lower border of the spine of the scapula. Here, the middle muscle bundles are contracting not only to lift his arm but also to produce power to take her extra weight – or part of it at least. The anterior muscle bundles, also contracting, are pulling the arm forward. The three parts insert into the deltoid tuberosity of the humerus.

The biceps and brachialis are both contracting to create strong forms as they bend his elbow and maintain joint stability.

The brachioradialis, spanning between the lower end of the radius at the wrist to the humerus, is also contracting to flex the elbow. It is called the carrying muscle, as it is used to carry weights.

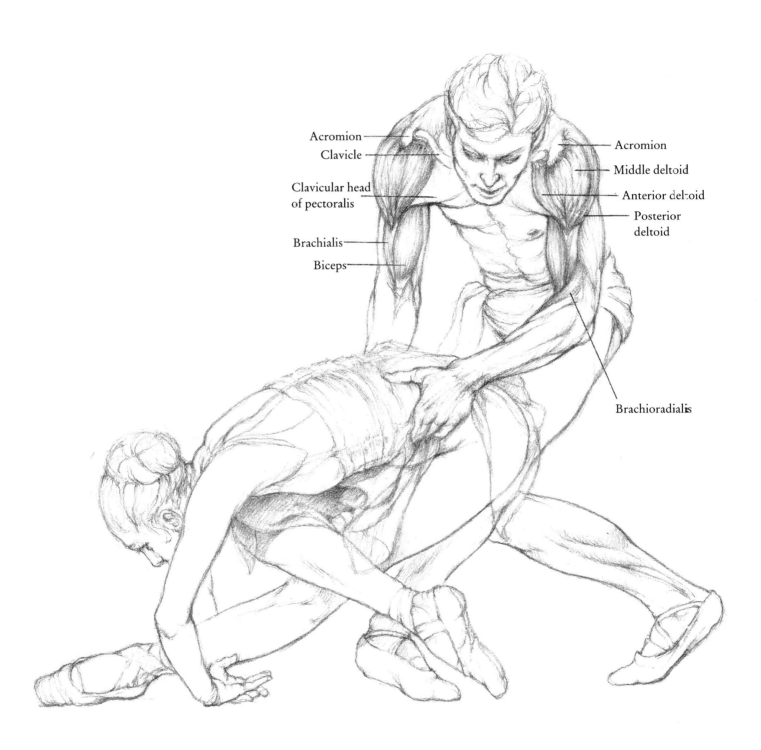

Acromion

Clavicle

Clavicular head
of pectoralis

Brachialis

Biceps

Acromion

Middle deltoid

Anterior deltoid

Posterior
deltoid

Brachioradialis

As a muscle contracts it produces movement. It also gives security to the joint, so it is performing both external and internal work. Some muscles too have to work against gravity as do the muscles at the back of the hip, the front of the thigh and the back of the leg as they are used to raise one from a sitting position to a standing one. Therefore they are larger and capable of exerting more power.

When a muscle is being used to lift or sustain a weight against gravity its optimum angle of pull (when it is acting with its greatest power) is a right angle. When the angle of pull departs from the right angle the internal work of holding the joint together begins to be performed and the lifting power is lessened.

In the case of the male dancer who is both lifting and sustaining a position, for a partner, there is a greater development in those mucles involved. The middle part of the deltoid which is used in raising the humerus, the biceps spanning between the scapula and the radius, which is used to bend (flex) the elbow, the brachialis spanning between the humerus and the ulna, which is used to flex the elbow, and the brachioradialis spanning from the lower part of the shaft of the humerus to the styloid process of the radius.

Middle
part
of deltoid

Biceps
Brachialis
Brachio-
radialis

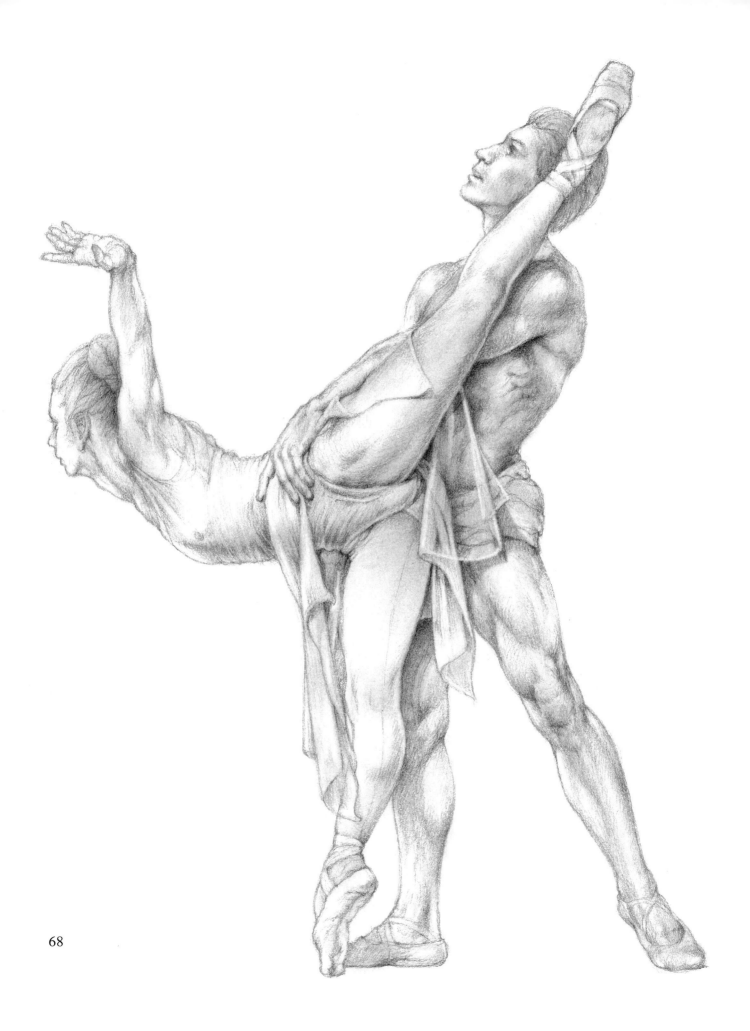

Landmarks for seated figure with arms upraised

The olecranon process of the ulna.

The medial epicondyle of the humerus

The bulk of the fleshy part of the triceps muscle and the flattened tendon going toward its insertion into the olecranon.

The scapular form with the latissimus dorsi over it.

The suprasternal notch.

The convex form of the rib cage.

The cartilaginous border of the rib cage.

The anterior superior spines.

The movement of the inguinal ligaments going from the anterior superior spines downward and medially to the pubis. This is the lower line of the abdomen.

The rounded form of the medial condyle of the femur and the sharp edge of the lateral condyle of the femur.

The patella which is shifting slightly to the lateral side when the knee is bent.

All of these landmarks can be palpated and seen on yourself.

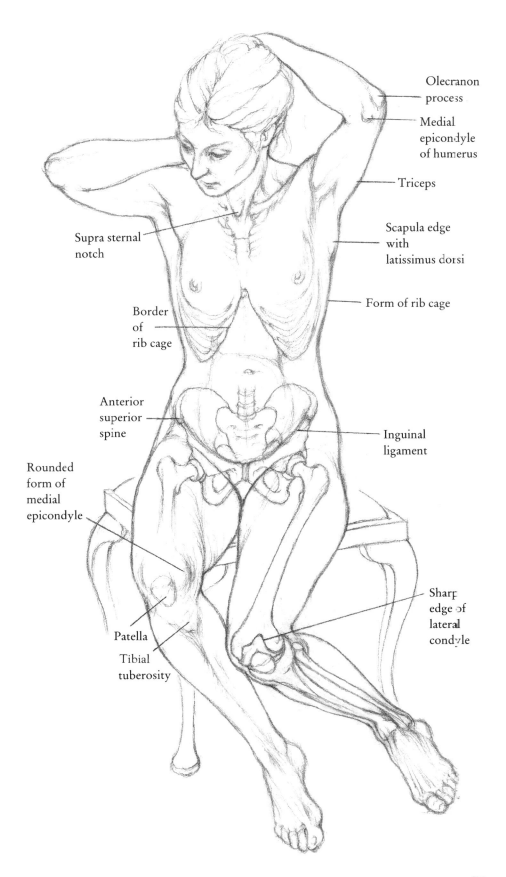

Olecranon
process

Medial
epicondyle
of humerus

Triceps

Scapula edge
with
latissimus dorsi

Form of rib cage

Supra sternal
notch

Border
of
rib cage

Anterior
superior
spine

Inguinal
ligament

Rounded
form of
medial
epicondyle

Sharp
edge of
lateral
condyle

Patella

Tibial
tuberosity

The light source is from above and to the right of her right side. Her left side is the shadow side turning away from the light. This includes the side plane of her head and neck, the torso, and areas on the arms and legs. The thighs are almost at a right angle to the torso and so receive light on their upper surfaces.

The shadow is deepened to the edge, with no line used on the edge, in some places on her left side. Reflected light which is not as bright shows the plane under her chin and on her left hip.

The light areas which are the same brightness as the background, on her arms and down the right side of her torso are delineated by line. Instead of line one could put in tone to her body edge, or in painting, colour.

Measurements and perspective

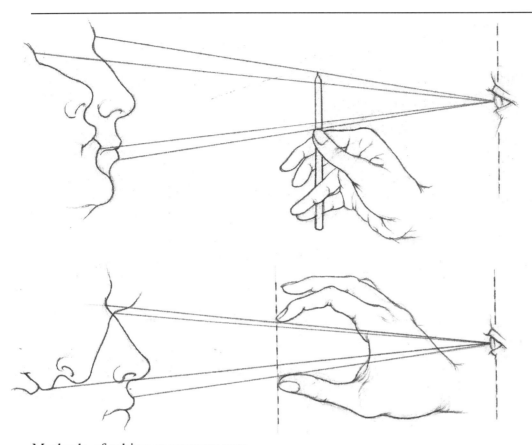

Methods of taking measurements
1 The arm is held directly out in front with the elbow kept rigid.
2 A pencil, or the imaginary line of the 'claw' between thumb and index finger is kept parallel (in the same plane as) your face, which is in turn parallel with the model.

For example:
If you are looking at a model you can quickly take the distance between the top of the head and the bottom of the chin, and then either with pencil or claw, move down in the same parallel line to see how many 'heads' are in that pose. There happen to be slightly over seven in this pose. If the perspective were different there would be more or fewer 'heads'. Tick the line to which the feet will come. The great toe is about seven heads. Put a light perpendicular line down the page as shown. Taking the head measurement again go across from the perpendicular to see how many heads the toe is from it, and tick there. It is about three and a half heads on this figure. The knee point (patella) is about three heads across and three heads down. With only a few basic measurements which have relation to the head and the pertinent ticks on the page the figure can be roughed in and developed in proportion.

74

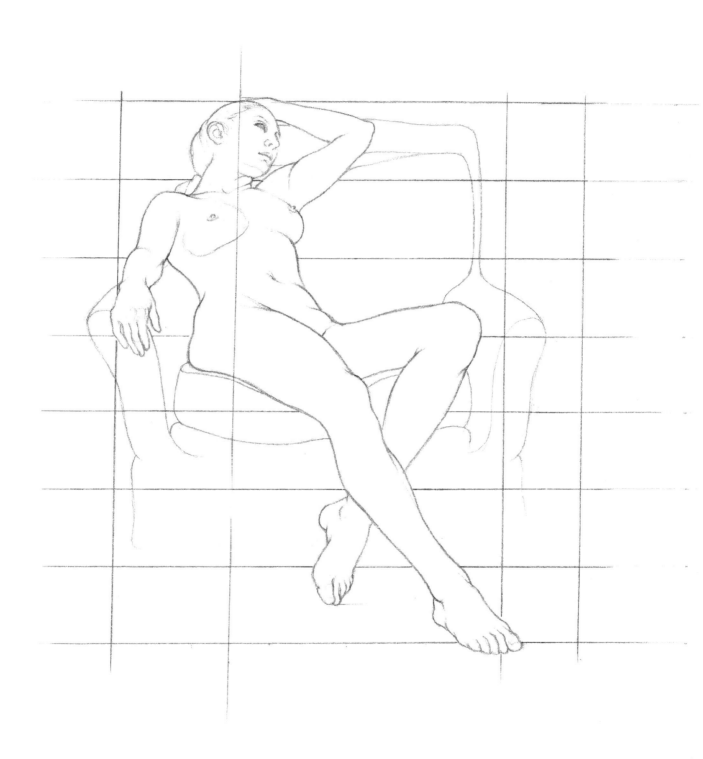

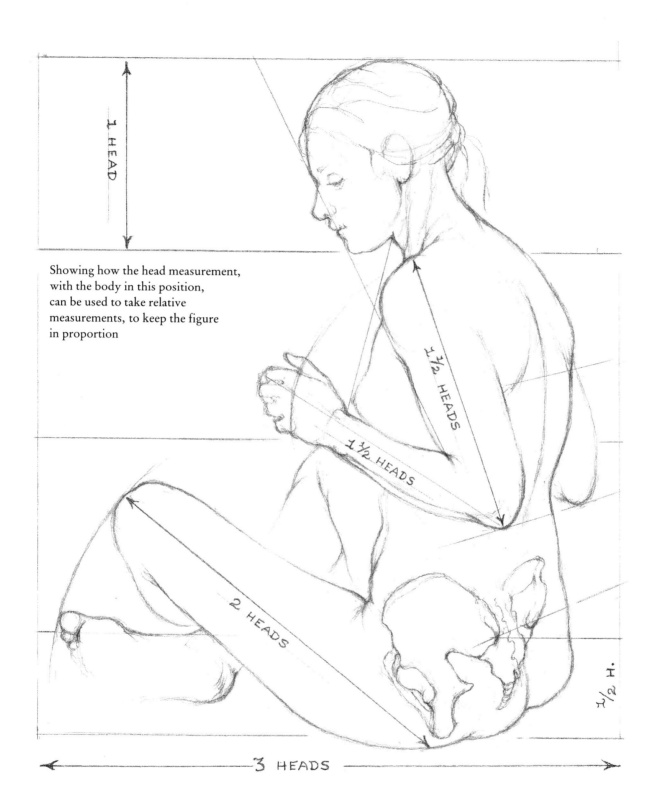

1 HEAD

Showing how the head measurement,
with the body in this position,
can be used to take relative
measurements, to keep the figure
in proportion

1 ½ HEADS

1 ½ HEADS

2 HEADS

½ H.

3 HEADS

76

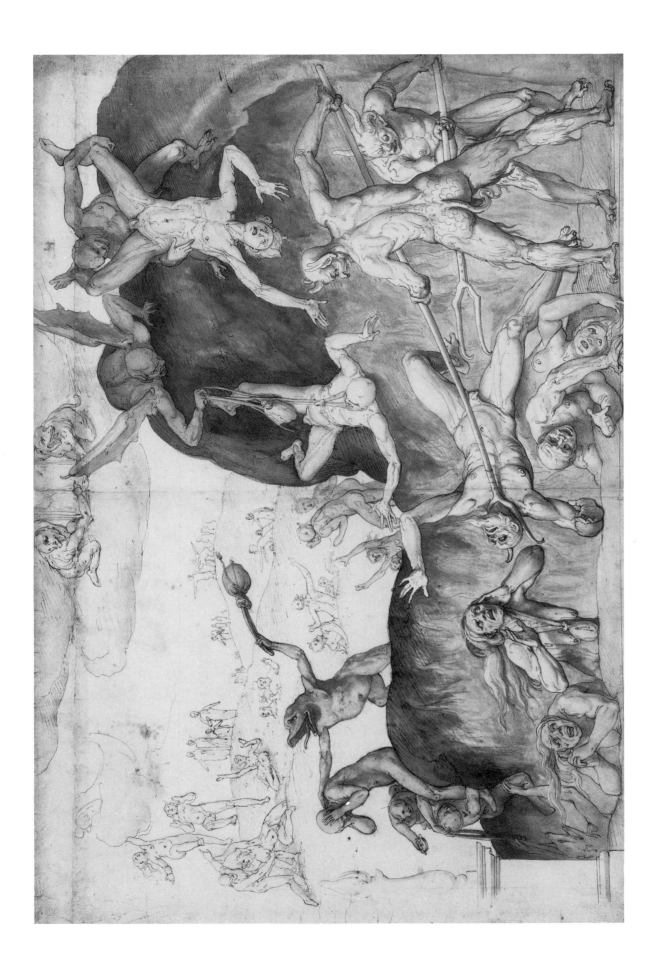

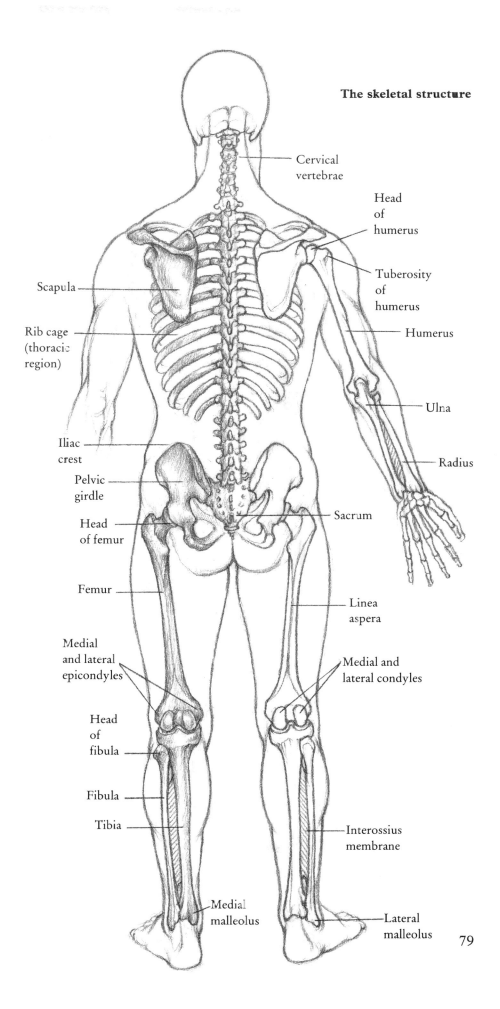

Cervical
vertebrae

Head
of
humerus

Tuberosity
of
humerus

Humerus

Scapula

Rib cage
(thoracic
region)

Ulna

Radius

Iliac
crest

Pelvic
girdle

Sacrum

Head
of femur

Femur

Linea
aspera

Medial
and lateral
epicondyles

Medial and
lateral condyles

Head
of
fibula

Fibula

Tibia

Interossius
membrane

Medial
malleolus

Lateral
malleolus

◄ *The punishment of*
Avaricious
Federico Zuccaro
1560–1590
By courtesy of British Museum

The muscles of the lower leg, posterior aspect

The SOLEUS and the GASTROCNEMIUS are the two muscles whose forms can be seen on the back of the lower leg.

The SOLEUS lies beneath the gastrocnemius but the forms of its lateral and medial margins can be seen, especially on the lateral side of the leg. This is worth noting as the form on the lateral side is therefore different from the medial side. The soleus is a large flat muscle attached to the upper one-fourth and head of the fibula, to a fibrous band which stretches between fibula and tibia, and from the medial one-third of the medial border of the tibia. It acts with the gastrocnemius. The tendon of the soleus joins that of the gastrocnemius to form the achilles tendon which inserts into the calcaneum (heel bone).

The GASTROCNEMIUS is the large superficial muscle which is responsible for the principle form on the back of the lower leg. It has two bellies and therefore two heads. These are tendinous attachments to the femur above its medial and lateral condyles, and they are large and flat. They span the back of the knee joint. The two fleshy bellies end in one large flat tendon which blends with the tendon of the soleus to form the achilles tendon. This tendon creates a straight, taut form from the calcaneum to the area of the muscle bundles. There is an apparent change of form in this region especially in athletic persons whose leg muscles are well developed. Also, the demarcation between the two bellies is often seen as an indentation.

The SOLEUS and the GASTROCNEMIUS are the chief plantar flexors of the foot. When their muscle bundles contract they bring the heel up and the sole of the foot (the plantar aspect) into view. They are the propulsive force in walking and jumping and will always be seen as thickened definite forms when the front part of the foot is pressed to the ground and the heel is raised.

Adding to the bulk at the back of the leg are three deep muscles which arise from the tibia and fibula and whose tendons pass into the foot behind the medial malleolus, using it as a pulley. Their long narrow tendons can create forms here which is worth noting.

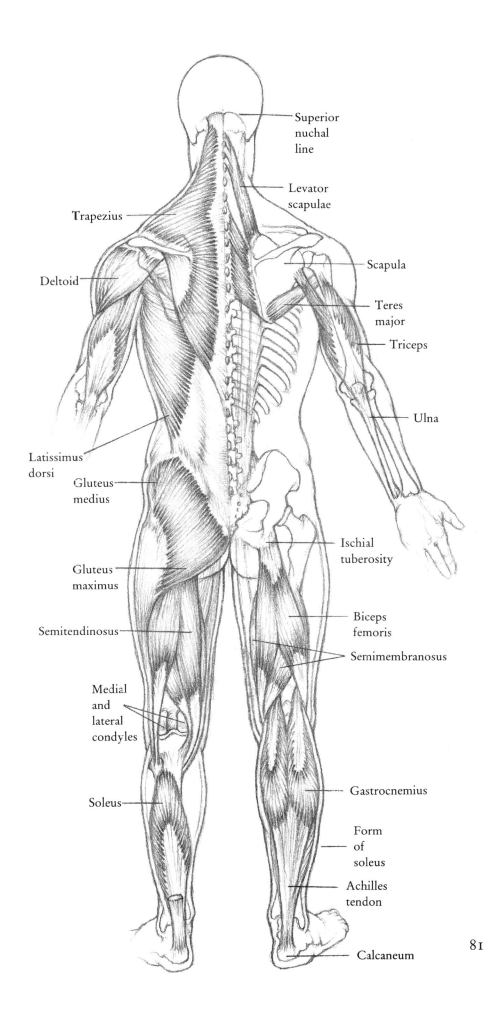

Superior
nuchal
line

Levator
scapulae

Trapezius

Scapula

Deltoid

Teres
major

Triceps

Ulna

Latissimus
dorsi

Gluteus
medius

Ischial
tuberosity

Gluteus
maximus

Biceps
femoris

Semitendinosus

Semimembranosus

Medial
and
lateral
condyles

Soleus

Gastrocnemius

Form
of
soleus

Achilles
tendon

Calcaneum

The muscles of the back

The two SACROSPINALES which attach to the sacrum and to the skull and to structures between these two points are the long unifying muscles for the action of the vertebral column. They are seen as long columns either side of the vertebrae, and are particularly prominent in the lumbar area.

The SACROSPINALIS muscle has a large flat tendinous attachment to the sacrum and the posterior part of the iliac crest. The pair of tendons create here a large flat triangular form on the buttocks over the sacral region. The muscle splits into three parts in the lumbar region, called spinalis, longissimus and ilio-costo-cervicalis.

The spinalis is a small part attaching to the spines of the lumbar and thoracic vertebrae.

The longissimus is attached to all the lumbar spines (5), all the thoracic spines (12) and to the lower ten ribs. Part continues to attach to the transverse processes of the second to the sixth cervical vertebrae. Yet another part continues to the skull to insert into the posterior margin of the mastoid process. Longissimus ties together the skull, vertebrae, ribs, sacrum and pelvis, an incredible unifying design.

The ilio-costo-cervicalis is inserted into the ribs and into the transverse processes of the fourth to the sixth cervical vertebrae. By its attachment to all the ribs it integrates the whole rib cage with the actions of the spine.

When both the SACROSPINALES contract, the vertebral column is bent backward (extension of the vertebral column) and the long columns of muscles will be seen mounding up over the midline especially in the lumbar region. When one of the pair contract, the trunk is bent laterally (to that side).

The QUADRATUS LUMBORUM is a short, thick column of muscle arising from the posterior part of the iliac crest and inserting into the transverse processes of the lumbar vertebrae, and the twelfth rib. Its origin is wider than its insertion into the rib so its lateral border is at an angle. Its mass and power is added to the sacrospinalis.

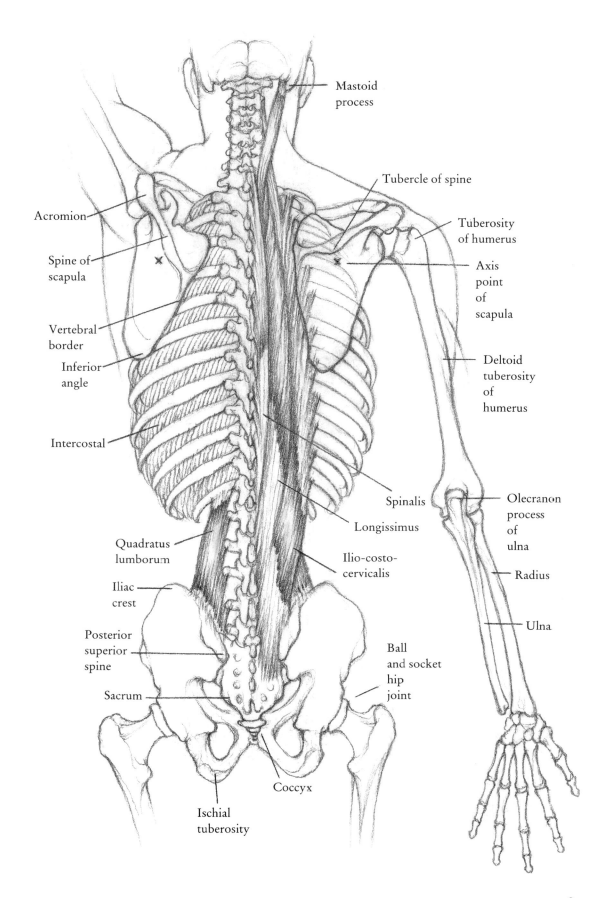

Mastoid
process

Tubercle of spine

Acromion

Tuberosity
of humerus

Spine of
scapula

Axis
point
of
scapula

Vertebral
border

Deltoid
tuberosity
of
humerus

Inferior
angle

Intercostal

Spinalis

Olecranon
process
of
ulna

Longissimus

Quadratus
lumborum

Ilio-costo-
cervicalis

Radius

Iliac
crest

Ulna

Posterior
superior
spine

Ball
and socket
hip
joint

Sacrum

Coccyx

Ischial
tuberosity

The scapula

The SCAPULA is a very important bone of the skeleton for the artist to understand as its design is complicated, it has many muscles attaching to it, and it also takes many positions with the different actions involving it.

It is a triangular flat bone, slightly arched from top to bottom to fit against the rib cage. With the clavicle it forms the pectoral girdle as it has a joint with the clavicle. The superior angle reaches to the second rib. The inferior angle which is strong and thickened bone due to muscles attachments usually reaches to the level of the seventh rib. The lateral angle has a shallow socket, the glenoid fossa, with which the head of the humerus articulates.

Across the back of the scapula there is a diagonal bar of bone which is called the spine of the scapula. It extends into a flattened free projection called the acromion process. The acromion can be felt on your own shoulder when the arm is relaxed. The fingers can be put around the tip of it, the upper surface palpated because it is just under the skin, and the bar of the spine can be felt angling downward across the back, as it too is subcutaneous. These are landmark points to look for on the surface. There is also a small finger-like process called the coracoid process which extends from the front of the scapula to provide attachment for the biceps and coracobrachialis muscles.

The scapula is rather like a raft on the back, even with its joint with the clavicle, because that joint can move. The scapula can be pulled in all directions by the muscles which pull on it like ropes. It is capable of movements up and down on the rib cage as in shrugging the shoulders, backward and forward rotation on its own axis, and greater movements of rotation in being pulled forward or backward, as the arms move.

In these movements look for three landmarks.

1 The spine with its acromion changing its angle as the scapula swings.
2 The inferior angle, seen as a rounded tapering form moving under the latissimus dorsi which lies over the angle.
3 The vertebral border, sometimes seen as a form lifting off the rib cage, and sometimes deep in a furrow when the arm is drawn back and the contracting muscles bury it.

The scapulae vary in size and shape (short, long, wide, narrow) from person to person.

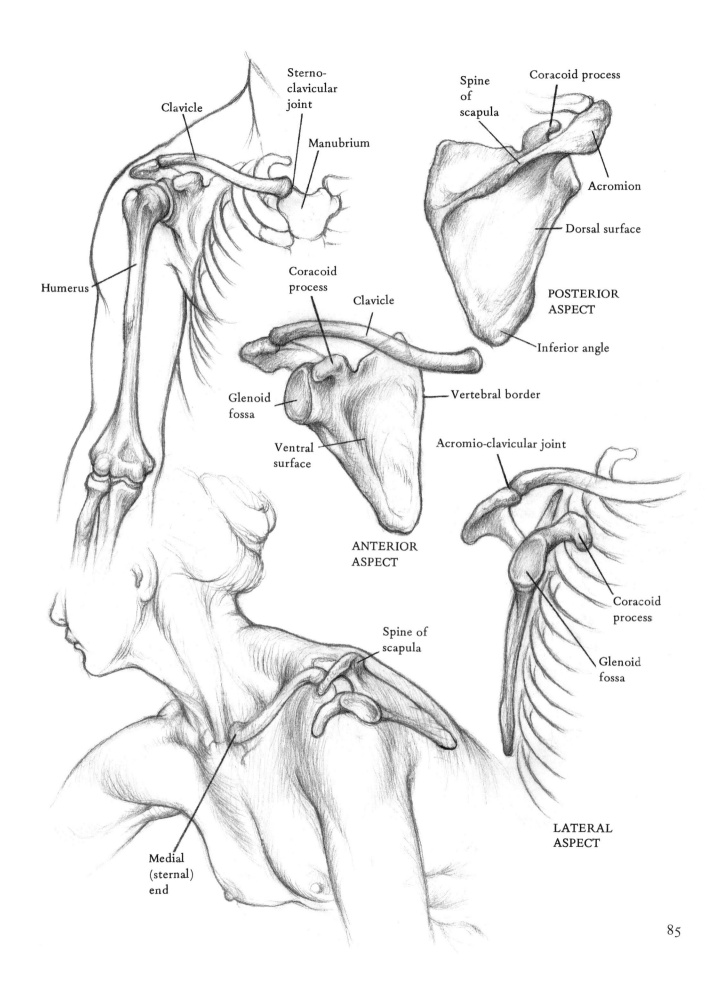

Clavicle

Sterno-
clavicular
joint

Manubrium

Spine
of
scapula

Coracoid process

Acromion

Dorsal surface

POSTERIOR
ASPECT

Inferior angle

Humerus

Coracoid
process

Clavicle

Glenoid
fossa

Vertebral border

Ventral
surface

ANTERIOR
ASPECT

Acromio-clavicular joint

Coracoid
process

Glenoid
fossa

Spine of
scapula

LATERAL
ASPECT

Medial
(sternal)
end

85

Muscles of the back

The SPLENIUS (meaning bandage) wraps around the side of the neck. It arises from the ligamentum nuchae and from the spines of the first six thoracic vertebrae. It spirals upward, attaching partly to the transverse processes of the first four cervical vertebrae, and partly to the posterior margin of the mastoid process. When it contracts, the head is drawn to that side and rotated, so the face is turned to that side.

The SERRATUS POSTERIOR SUPERIOR arises from the lower cervical and the upper thoracic spines and inserts into the second to fifth ribs.

The SERRATUS POSTERIOR INFERIOR arises from the lower thoracic and upper lumbar spines and is inserted into the ninth to twelfth ribs. Both of these muscles are used to stretch the rib cage when one breathes in.

The RHOMBOID MINOR arises from the lower part of the ligamentum nuchae and from the spines of the seventh cervical and first thoracic vertebrae. It is inserted into the vertebral border of the scapula at the root of the spine.

The RHOMBOID MAJOR arises from the spines of the second, third, fourth and fifth thoracic vertebrae. It is inserted into the vertebral border of the scapula between the root of the spine and the inferior angle. The rhomboids pull the scapula upward and backward as the direction of their muscle bundles indicate. Their forms can be seen in those with developed back muscles, bulging under the trapezius which lies over them, and with which they share work. They, with the trapezius, are responsible for the mounding up of flesh between the vertebral border of the scapula and the vertebral column, when the arms are drawn back. If the vertebral column is being bent backward at that time also, the spinales will add to that mound, and the border of the scapula will be in a furrow.

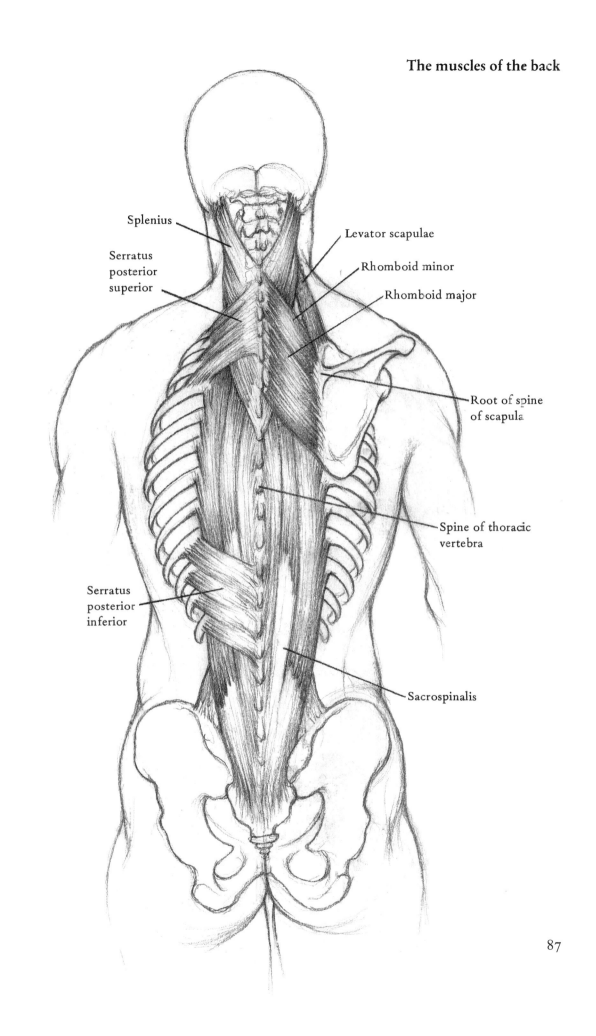

Splenius

Serratus
posterior
superior

Levator scapulae

Rhomboid minor

Rhomboid major

Root of spine
of scapula

Spine of thoracic
vertebra

Serratus
posterior
inferior

Sacrospinalis

The LEVATOR SCAPULAE arises from the transverse processes of the first four cervical vertebrae and is inserted into the upper part of the medial border (the vertebral border) of the scapula. It acts with the trapezius to lift the scapula, and the inferior angle of the scapula swings slightly to the midline also, when it contracts.

The TRAPEZIUS is a triangular sheet of muscle covering the top of the shoulder, the back of the neck and the medial part of the thorax. It arises from the medial one-third of the superior nuchal line of the skull. Its muscle bundles pass in three directions. The upper ones pass downward and laterally from the skull to insert into the flattened lateral third of the clavicle. The middle ones pass almost horizontally to insert into the upper border of the spine of the scapula and the medial margin of the acromion. The whole top of the shoulder is this covered by the trapezius and gives it its form. The lower muscle bundles pass upward and insert into the lower border of the spine of the scapula, and its tubercle. As the scapula rotates forward the upper muscle bundles are contracting to raise the point of the shoulder, while the lower bundles pull down the spine. In full rotation the upper bundles are in full contraction, mounded up on the shoulder, while the lower bundles are stretched and flat against the rib cage.

The LATISSIMUS DORSI has a broad aponeurotic origin extending from the seventh thoracic vertebra (under cover of the trapezius), all the lumbar and sacral spines, and to the lateral part of the iliac crest from the posterior superior spine area. An aponeurosis greatly increases the possibility of more attachment for fleshy muscle. It also has its origin from the three lower ribs. This great flat mass of muscle converges upward, taking a complete turn on itself to insert into the humerus on its anterior side. The resulting thick rolled edge of it can be seen leaving the rib cage area to span across to the arm. Like the pectoralis, its lowest edge of origin rolls under to become the highest edge to insert. It forms the heavy mass at the back of the arm pit. The latissimus dorsi is used in all those actions where the arm is brought back. It rotates the humerus forward in its socket. If one is hanging suspended by the hands, the latissimus is the chief muscle in enabling the body to be raised. The inferior angle of the scapula is covered by the latissimus dorsi and is held to the rib cage by it.

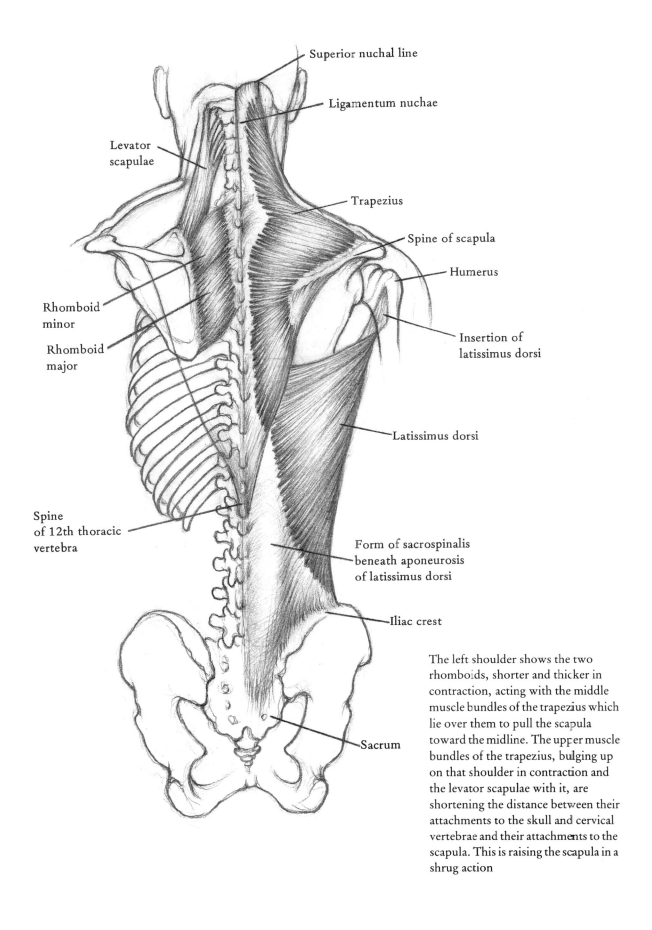

Superior nuchal line

Ligamentum nuchae

Levator
scapulae

Trapezius

Spine of scapula

Humerus

Rhomboid
minor

Rhomboid
major

Insertion of
latissimus dorsi

Latissimus dorsi

Spine
of 12th thoracic
vertebra

Form of sacrospinalis
beneath aponeurosis
of latissimus dorsi

Iliac crest

Sacrum

The left shoulder shows the two
rhomboids, shorter and thicker in
contraction, acting with the middle
muscle bundles of the trapezius which
lie over them to pull the scapula
toward the midline. The upper muscle
bundles of the trapezius, bulging up
on that shoulder in contraction and
the levator scapulae with it, are
shortening the distance between their
attachments to the skull and cervical
vertebrae and their attachments to the
scapula. This is raising the scapula in a
shrug action

The dorsal surface of the scapula and the upper arm

The scapula is clothed with four muscles on its dorsal surface. They all insert into the humerus in the upper part of its shaft, its greater tuberosity, by tendon.

The SUPRASPINATUS arises above the spine of the scapula. Its muscle bundles converge under the acromion and its tendon inserts into the highest part of the tuberosity. It assists the deltoid in raising the arm and is covered by the trapezius.

The INFRASPINATUS arises from a large part of the dorsal surface of the scapula, just below the spine. It is a thick muscle and its rounded form is seen bounded by the trapezius and deltoid. It acts with the posterior part of the deltoid to pull the arm back and rotate the head of the humerus backward.

The TERES MINOR arises from the lateral border of the scapula and inserts into the tuberosity just below the infraspinatus. It helps rotate the humerus backward.

The TERES MAJOR arises from the dorsal surface of the inferior angle of the scapula. It passes across the armpit to attach on the anterior side of the humerus. The muscle therefore when it contracts rotates the head of the humerus forward in its socket, and pulls the humerus back. In a person with well developed muscles the forms of these last three can be seen clearly. Otherwise they appear as one or two forms, slightly rounded on the surface, above the upper border of the latissimus dorsi.

The SUBSCAPULARIS, not seen on the surface because it is on the ventral side of the scapula, covers the whole surface. Its tendon inserts into the anterior aspect of the tuberosity.

These five muscles are known as the 'rotator cuff' as they control the action of the head of the humerus rotating in the socket.

The TRICEPS, as its name indicates, has three heads. Two of them are attached to the shaft of the humerus, the medial head lying under the other two, and the long head spanning the back of the armpit to attach to the scapula just under the glenoid fossa. They have a common flat tendon which appears as a flattened area on the back of the upper arm above the elbow. This tendon spans the elbow joint and inserts into the olecranon process of the ulna, which can be seen on the surface. The triceps is the only muscle on the back of the upper arm and is the great extensor of it, straightening the elbow joint.

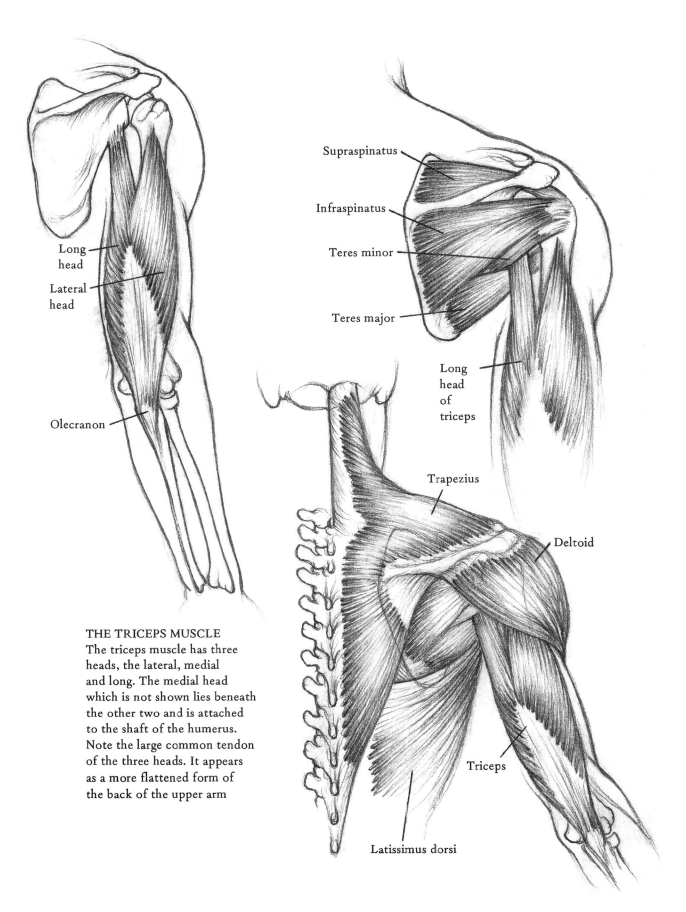

Supraspinatus

Infraspinatus

Teres minor

Teres major

Long
head
of
triceps

Long
head

Lateral
head

Olecranon

Trapezius

Deltoid

Triceps

Latissimus dorsi

THE TRICEPS MUSCLE
The triceps muscle has three
heads, the lateral, medial
and long. The medial head
which is not shown lies beneath
the other two and is attached
to the shaft of the humerus.
Note the large common tendon
of the three heads. It appears
as a more flattened form of
the back of the upper arm

In the following figure:

The arms are being strongly extended backward. The triceps fleshy and contracting heads are emerging from under the posterior part of the deltoid. The forms of two parts of the deltoid, the middle and posterior, can be seen. The middle part is puckering because of its septa. The posterior parts are the strong rounded bands leading from the spine area of the scapula over to the humerus. On his left side, the deltoid has a richer form and is more strongly puckered because it is raising that arm slightly higher, with more muscle bundles in its middle part contracting.

Both the scapulae are being pulled back to the midline of the back. Their vertebral borders are deep in the two furrows which lead down to their inferior angles. His left inferior angle is higher because that scapula is being pulled up toward the head. This action is caused by the trapezius contracting and it can be seen as a prominent mound on his left shoulder. Its contracting form leads right up to the skull.

Between the buried vertebral borders of the scapula and the midline, where the vertebrae are also buried, the two rhomboids are contracting and also the lower fleshy part of the trapezius, causing the mounds.

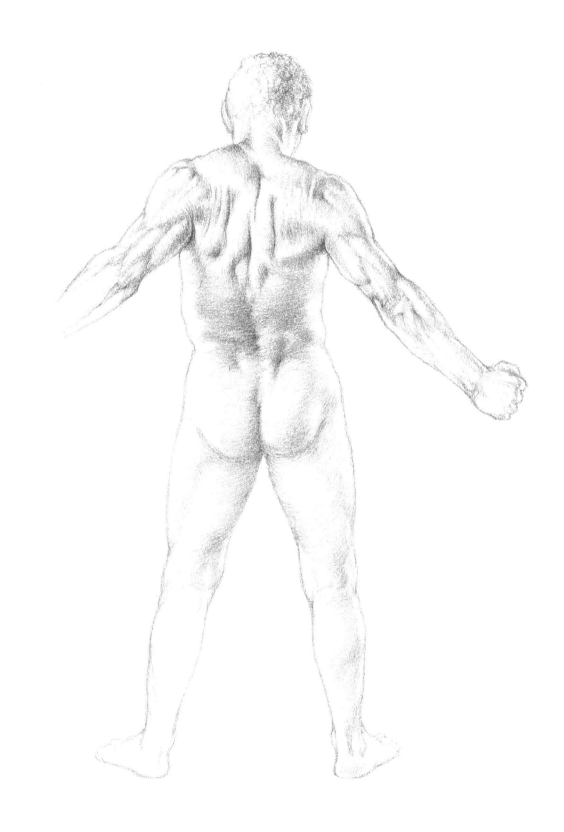

The following drawings show:

The lower muscles bundles of the trapezius are contracting and appear as definite small columns, either side of the midline of the back. The flat area between them is the aponeurotic tendinous attachment of the trapezius to the spines of the thoracic vertebrae. The middle and upper fleshy parts of the trapezius which are attached to the medial edge of the acromions and the upper borders of the spines of the scapulae are also very obvious mounds as the muscle works to rotate the scapulae. In full rotation of the scapulae, with the arms raised forward and high above the head, the whole lower part of the trapezius is stretched, and would appear quite flattened against the rib cage.

The deltoids are both contracting, lifting the upper arms. The biceps and brachialis muscles are working with them, both to lift the ulna and radius in the lower arms but mainly here to flex the arms against resistance.

The latissimus dorsi muscles are holding the inferior angles of the scapulae against the rib cage. The infraspinatus and the teres major are bulging forms over the upper edges of this muscle.

Note the form of the brachialis. It lies partially under the biceps and is a very powerful muscle. It has a V-shaped attachment on either side of the insertion of the deltoid into the deltoid tuberosity of the humerus, and it is crossing under the biceps to insert into the ulna. Also, on his left arm, the brachioradialis is working with the biceps and brachialis to strongly flex that arm against resistance.

The forms of both inferior angles of the scapulae can be seen. The left one is more apparent on the edge.

The quadratus lumborum and the spinalis on his right side are stronger contracting forms as he is bending slightly backward as well as to his right.

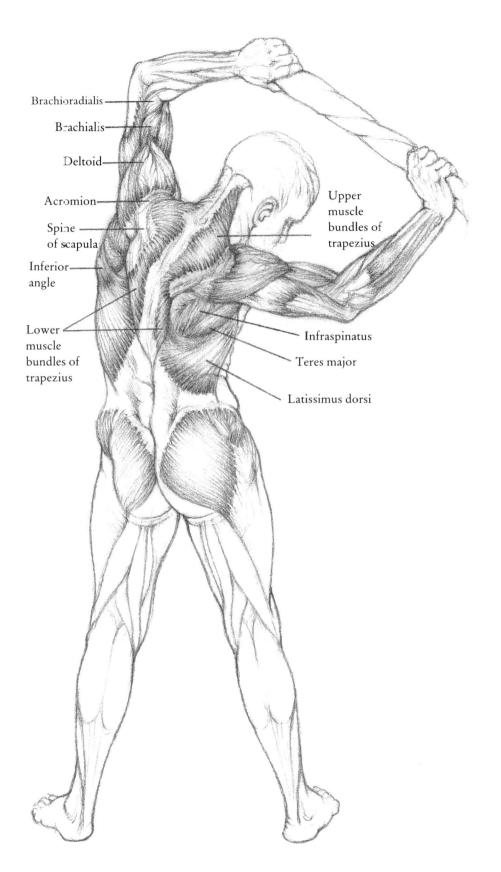

Brachioradialis

Brachialis

Deltoid

Acromion

Spine
of scapula

Inferior
angle

Lower
muscle
bundles of
trapezius

Upper
muscle
bundles of
trapezius

Infraspinatus

Teres major

Latissimus dorsi

95

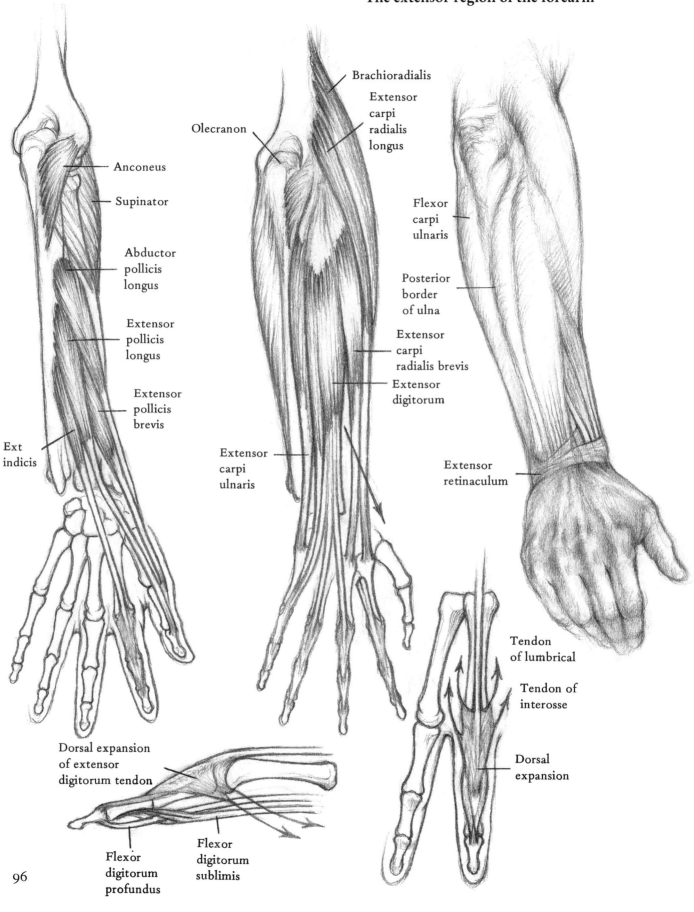

Anconeus

Supinator

Abductor
pollicis
longus

Extensor
pollicis
longus

Extensor
pollicis
brevis

Ext
indicis

Olecranon

Brachioradialis

Extensor
carpi
radialis
longus

Flexor
carpi
ulnaris

Posterior
border
of ulna

Extensor
carpi
radialis brevis

Extensor
digitorum

Extensor
carpi
ulnaris

Extensor
retinaculum

Tendon
of lumbrical

Tendon of
interosse

Dorsal
expansion

Dorsal expansion
of extensor
digitorum tendon

Flexor
digitorum
profundus

Flexor
digitorum
sublimis

96

The gluteus maximus, the tensor fasciae latae and the ilio-tibial tract

The TENSOR FASCIAE LATAE is a small muscle about 15 cm long which is attached to the anterior superior spine and adjacent iliac crest. It is inserted into the ilio-tibial tract.

The ILIO-TIBIAL TRACT is a part of the whole sheath of fascia which encloses the muscles of the thigh. Fascia is a sheet of fibrous tissue enveloping the body beneath the skin. That of the thigh is particularly strong and is called fascia lata. The fibres of the sheath run circularly but at the lateral side of the thigh there is a very strong band of fibres running longitudinally between the layers of circular. This band is called the ilio-tibial tract. This tract is important. It creates a taut band down the side of the thigh and there is an indentation or furrow caused by it. This is because the tract is attached along its length to the lateral intermuscular septum, a partition of fascia which is in turn attached along the length of the linea aspera at the posterior of the femur. Its furrow is apparent to varying degrees in most thighs. The tract is inserted into the lateral condyle of the tibia. When the tensor fasciae latae muscle contracts it tightens the tract and helps to straighten (extend) the knee. It is especially well developed in ballet dancers, as are the gluteus medius and gluteus maximus, where the full range of hip movement is used so constantly.

The GLUTEUS MAXIMUS is a large rhomboidal shaped muscle. It is attached to the posterior part of the iliac crest, the posterior superior spine, the side and back of the sacrum and the coccyx. The inner lower quarter of the muscle inserts into the femur. The remaining three-quarters is inserted into the ilio-tibial tract. Through this insertion the gluteus maximus becomes the powerful extensor of the knee, because the ilio-tibial tract is attached to the tibia in front of the axis of the knee.

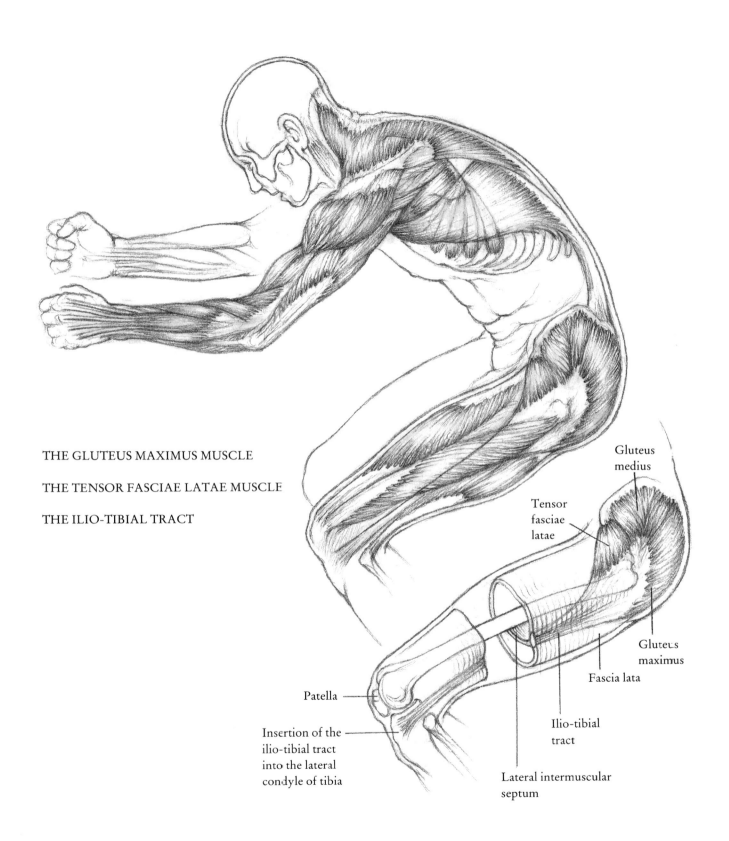

THE GLUTEUS MAXIMUS MUSCLE

THE TENSOR FASCIAE LATAE MUSCLE

THE ILIO-TIBIAL TRACT

Gluteus medius

Tensor fasciae latae

Gluteus maximus

Fascia lata

Ilio-tibial tract

Patella

Lateral intermuscular septum

Insertion of the ilio-tibial tract into the lateral condyle of tibia

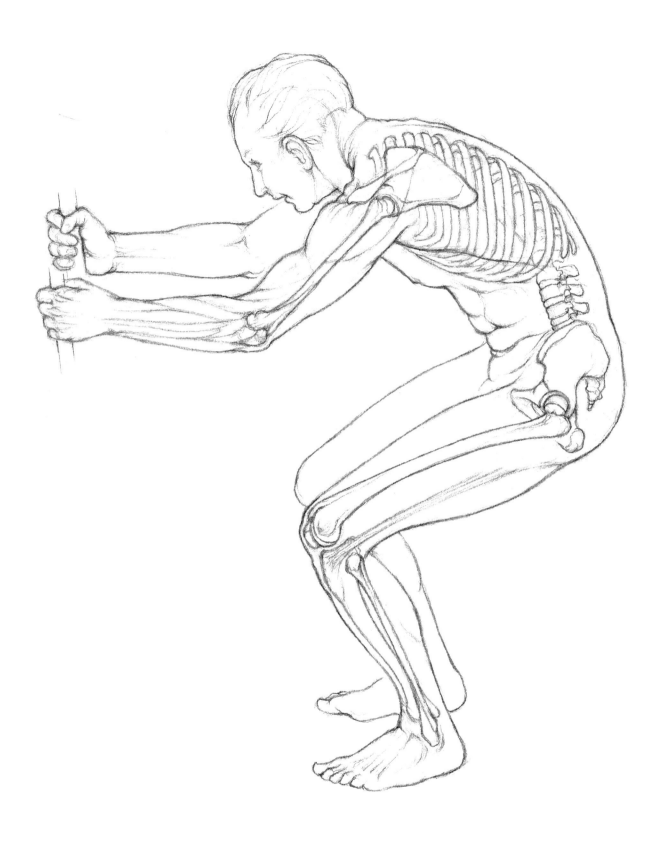

The hamstring muscles

These muscles are so named because if their tendons are cut behind the knee, the knee cannot be flexed to allow a step to be taken and a person is therefore powerless and is hamstrung.

There are three hamstring muscles, BICEPS FEMORIS which has two heads, SEMIMEMBRANOSUS and SEMITENDINOSUS.

They have their origin from the ischial tuberosity of the pelvis, except for the shorter head of the biceps femoris which arises from the back of the femur.

The two heads of the biceps femoris are inserted into the head of the fibula by a common (one) tendon. Semimembranosus is inserted by a thick tendon into the medial condyle of the tibia. Semitendinosus passes from behind the knee, forward, to insert into the medial surface of the tibia.

The fleshy bellies of these muscles account for the rich rounded form filling the whole back of the thigh. The tendons can be felt on either side at the back of the knee and when the knee is bent (flexed) they account for the medial and lateral 'pillar' forms one sees at the back of the knee joint.

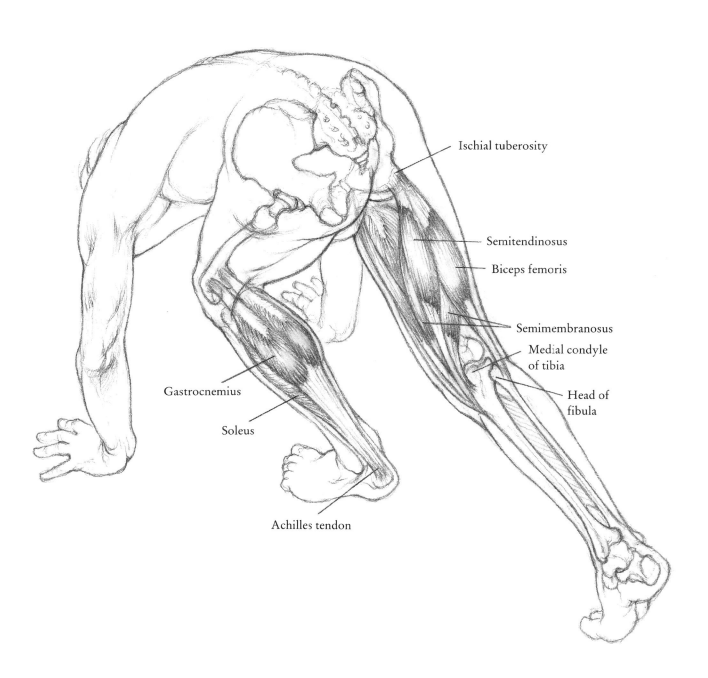

Ischial tuberosity

Semitendinosus

Biceps femoris

Semimembranosus

Medial condyle
of tibia

Head of
fibula

Gastrocnemius

Soleus

Achilles tendon

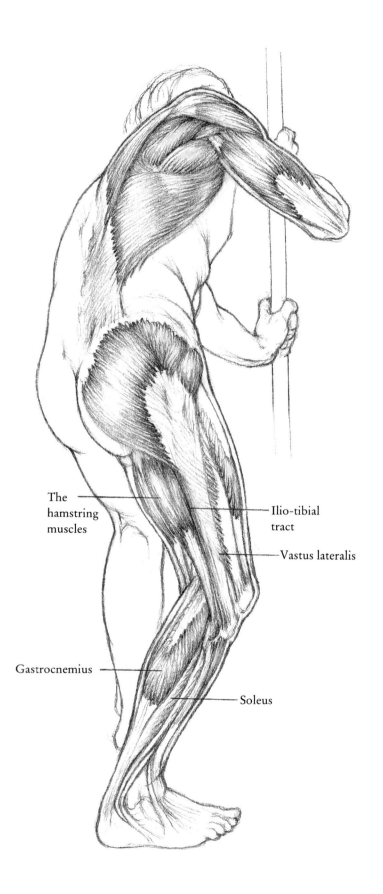

The
hamstring
muscles

Ilio-tibial
tract

Vastus lateralis

Gastrocnemius

Soleus

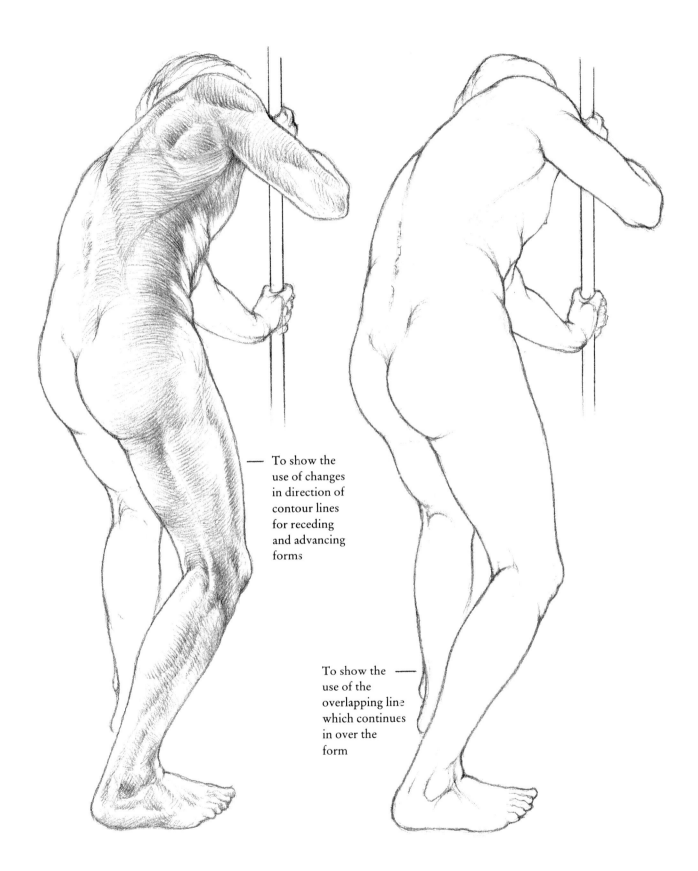

To show the
use of changes
in direction of
contour lines
for receding
and advancing
forms

To show the
use of the
overlapping line
which continues
in over the
form

Landmarks to help sketch the figure

1 Choose a point of reference. The one chosen here is the jaw line leading to the ear. Drop a perpendicular line to see the action of the figure both sides of that line. In this drawing it is in line with the right side of his right heel.

2 Take a measurement vertically from the chin to the top of the head. Use this measurement, as shown, the get the body in relationship with the head. In this sketch it is a little over six heads high.

   There is no need to put these measurement lines in as are shown. They can be done 'in the air' with either the claw method, and just ticking a mark lightly with a pencil, or by the pencil being used, held vertically in front of your eyes. In this stance there are approximately two head measurements from heel to heel, so the left heel position can be checked, and ticked in.

3 The landmarks to look for in this figure are:
   (a) The movement of the spine through the perpendicular.
   (b) The form of the thorax (rib cage).
   (c) The two scapulae on the rib cage.
   (d) The indentations (the dimples) on the buttocks where the posterior superior spines are situated.
   (e) The greater trochanter of the femur, at the hip.
   (f) The big rounded form of the hamstring muscles.
   (g) The rounded form of the gastrocnemii (the calf muscles) and the straight pull line of the achilles tendons to the heels.

Note the plane change on the head, from the small face area to the side and top planes of the cranium which are much bigger.

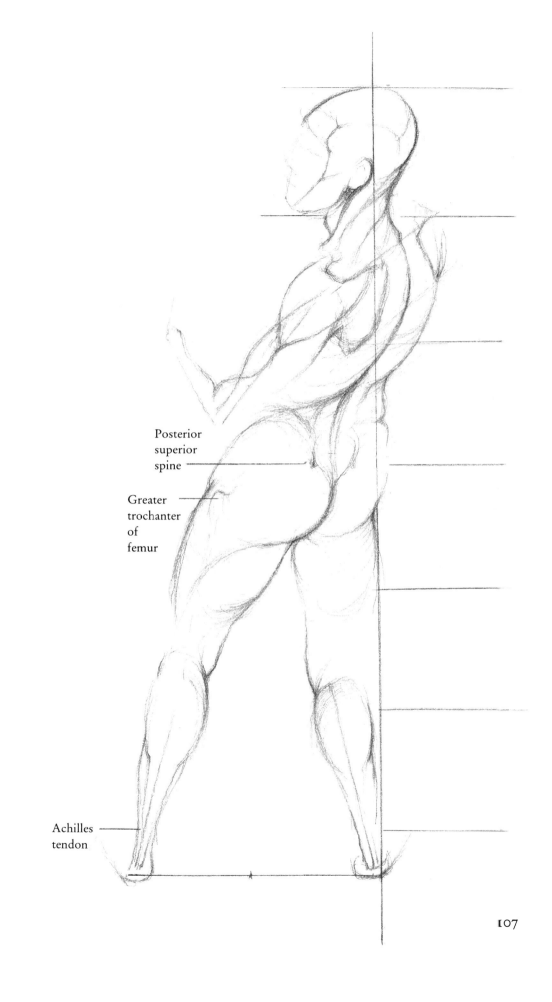

Posterior
superior
spine

Greater
trochanter
of
femur

Achilles
tendon

This action shows the upper muscle bundles of the trapezius covering the whole top of the shoulder. They have tendinous attachment to the superior nuchal line of the skull at the back, and some of them 'roll over' the shoulder creating a very strong form as they insert into the lateral one-third of the clavicle. Other bundles are inserted by tendinous fibres into the medial edge of the acromion and the upper border of the spine of the scapula. This part of the trapezius suspends the clavicle and scapula, which are called the pectoral girdle.

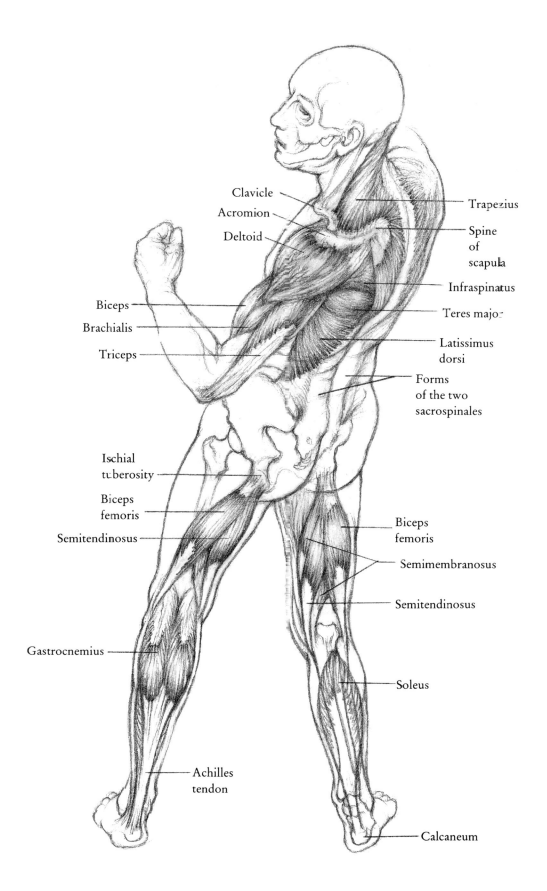

Clavicle

Acromion

Deltoid

Trapezius

Spine
of
scapula

Infraspinatus

Teres major

Biceps

Brachialis

Triceps

Latissimus
dorsi

Forms
of the two
sacrospinales

Ischial
tuberosity

Biceps
femoris

Semitendinosus

Biceps
femoris

Semimembranosus

Semitendinosus

Gastrocnemius

Soleus

Achilles
tendon

Calcaneum

109

The lumbar vertebrae are arching forward and rotating as the sacrospinales contract. The muscles are therefore very apparent columns in the lumbar region. The quadratus muscles beneath them will also be contracting and add even more form.

The sacrospinales on his left side is contracting more than the one on his right side, so the trunk is pulled to the left side.

The arm is being raised by the deltoid contracting, helped by the supraspinatus, and also it is being pulled forward.

The deltoid muscle is attached to the lateral flattened one-third of the clavicle, the lateral border of the acromion and from the lower edge of the spine of the scapula. Its tendon inserts and creates a roughened area on the humerus called the deltoid tuberosity. The muscle is divided into three parts, anterior, middle and posterior. The anterior part pulls the arm forward and the posterior part, backward. The middle part is used in raising the arm and the internal structure of this section is designed for this function. Four tendinous septa (partitions) descend from the acromion and short muscle bundles are attached to these diagonally, like barbs on a feather. It is therefore called a bipennate muscle. This structure of the deltoid is of great importance to the artist because when the muscle bundles are shorter and thicker in contraction, these septa appear like furrows in the form of the deltoid.

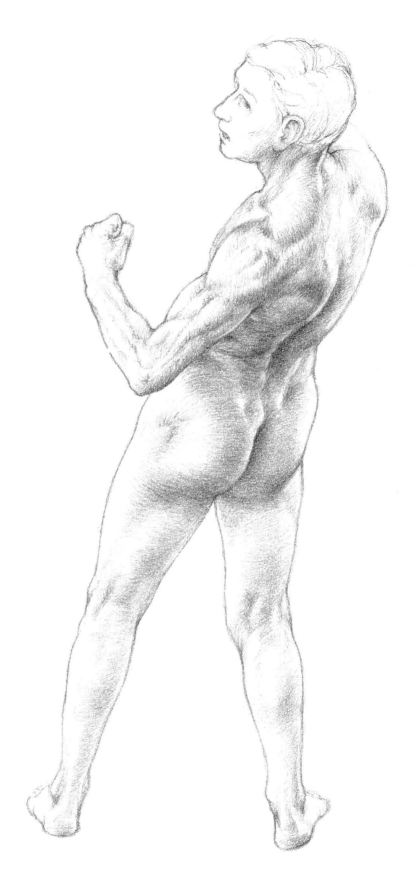

III

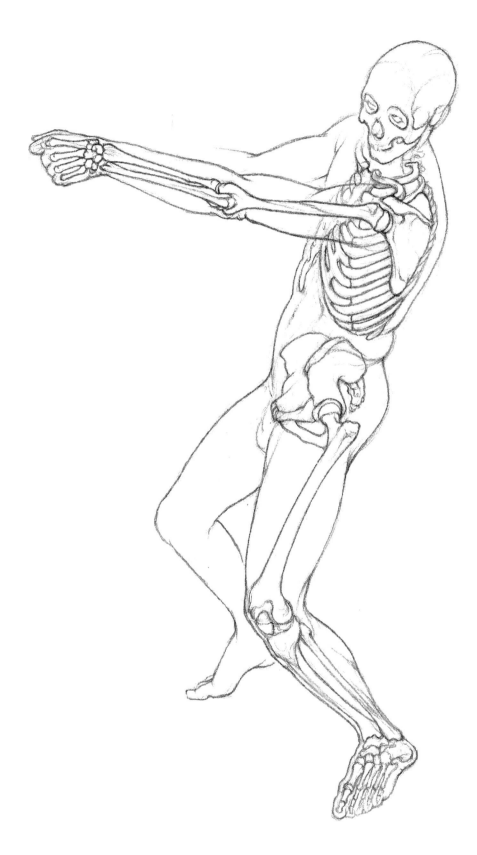

Muscles of the lower leg – lateral aspect

TIBIALIS ANTERIOR arises from the lateral surface of the tibia, the interosseus membrane whose fibres run downward and laterally and join tibia to fibula, and the upper two-thirds of the lateral surface of the tibia. Its strong tendon can be seen at the ankle and in the foot, passing obliquely medially and inserting into the first cuneiform bone and the first metatarsal on their medial sides.

EXTENSOR DIGITORUM LONGUS arises from the lateral condyle of the tibia, the interosseus membrane and the upper three-quarters of the anterior surface of the shaft of the fibula. Its tendon passes under the retinaculum, and then divides into four. These four tendons insert into the second, third, fourth and fifth toes.

PERONEUS TERTIUS arises from the lower one-third of the anterior surface of the fibula. Its tendon passes to insert into the upper part of the base of the fifth metatarsal. It raises the lateral side of the foot so man can walk four-square, but is not always present.

These three muscles pull the toes up. The great toes has its own muscle, the EXTENSOR HALLUCIS LONGUS whose tendon can be seen on you own foot, and is an important landmark.

PERONEUS LONGUS arises from the head of the fibula and the upper two-thirds of its lateral surface. Its long tendon runs obliquely backward to pass behind the lateral malleolus before entering the foot. It crosses under the arch to insert into the first metatarsal and the first cuneiform. It creates a kind of sling under the arch of the foot with tibialis anterior.

PERONEUS BREVIS arises from the lower two-thirds of the lateral surface of the fibula. Its tendon also passes behind the lateral malleolus and then goes forward to insert into the base of the fifth metatarsal. It works to keep the foot steady and level.

The oblique movement of these two muscles with the strong movement of their tendinous parts behind the lateral malleoli is important.

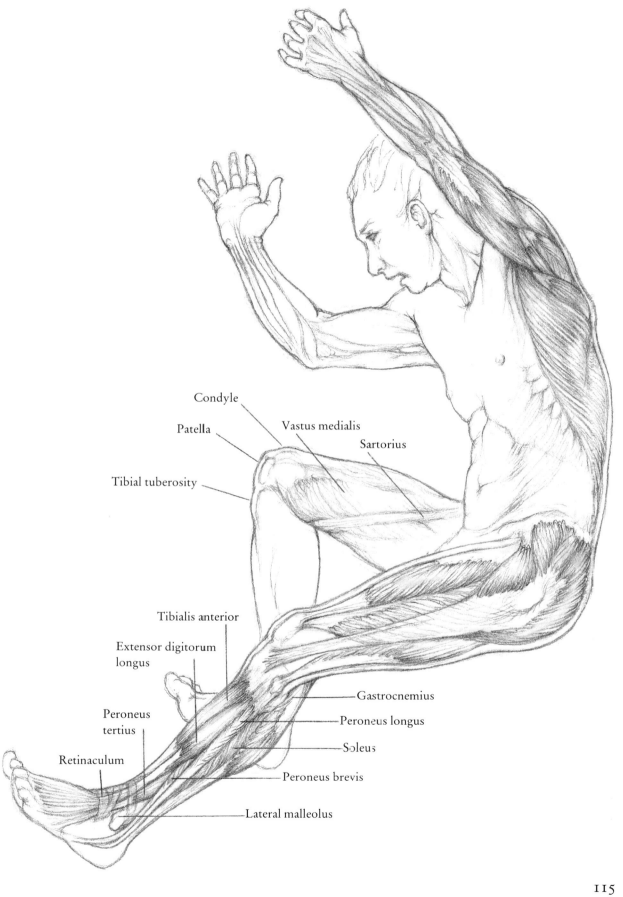

Condyle

Patella

Vastus medialis

Sartorius

Tibial tuberosity

Tibialis anterior

Extensor digitorum
longus

Gastrocnemius

Peroneus longus

Peroneus
tertius

Soleus

Retinaculum

Peroneus brevis

Lateral malleolus

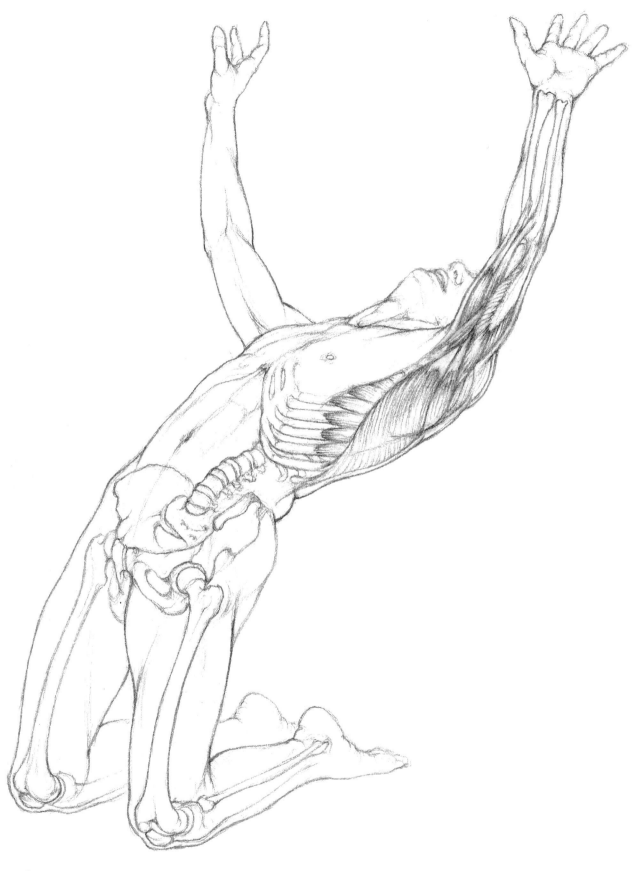

116

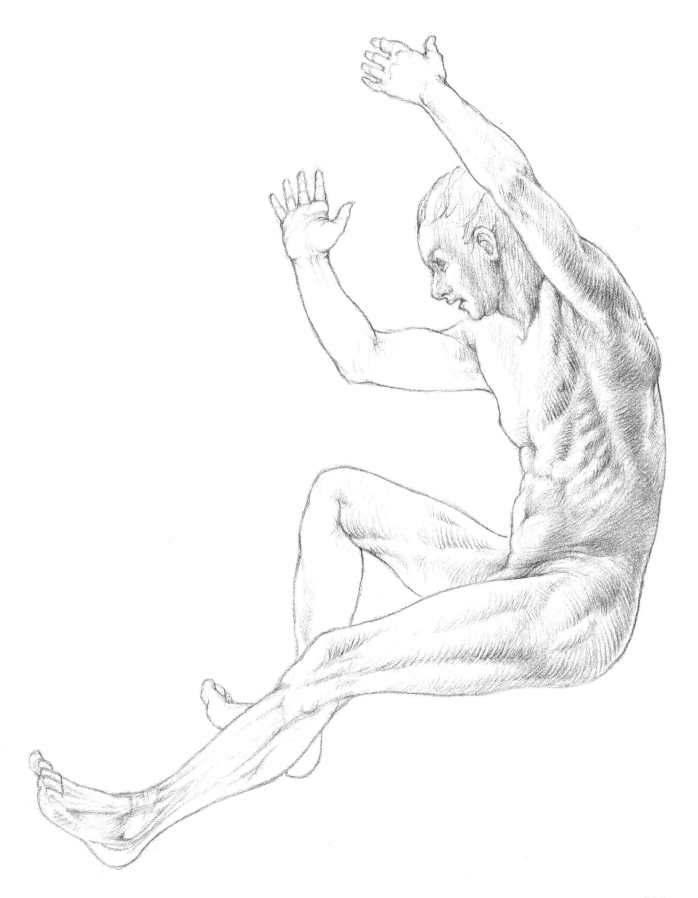

Landmarks to help sketch the figure

1 The perpendicular is dropped from the point where the ear lobe meets the jaw.
2 The trachea has a strong curve as it goes behind the suprasternal notch of the manubrium to enter the thorax.
3 The cartilaginous edge of the rib cage is an important form.
4 The anterior superior spine of the pelvis with the flesh bulging slightly over it.
5 The greater trochanter of the femur may be difficult to see but is worth looking for.
6 The fleshy part of the biceps femoris muscle is a rich form in contraction.
7 The ilio-tibial tract is a linear indentation.
8 The head of the fibula, where the biceps femoris is attached.
9 The patella, with a definite plane change from its top to its front surface.
10 The lateral malleolus of the fibula (the right outside ankle bone) which can always be seen.

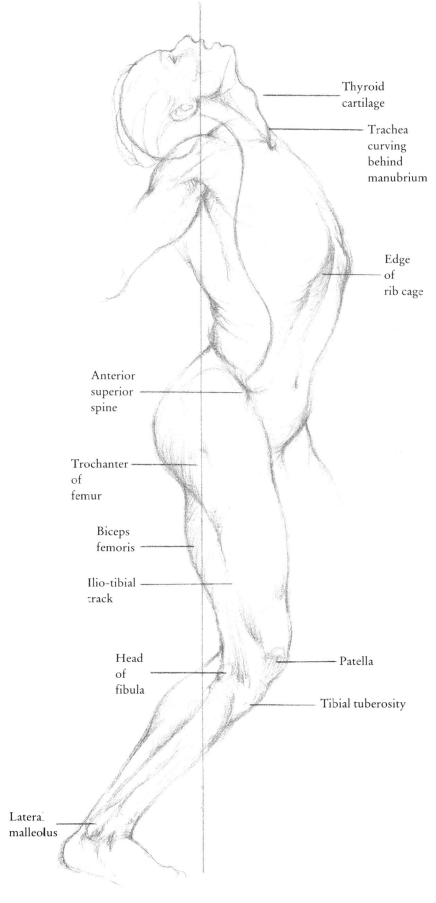

Thyroid
cartilage

Trachea
curving
behind
manubrium

Edge
of
rib cage

Anterior
superior
spine

Trochanter
of
femur

Biceps
femoris

Ilio-tibial
track

Head
of
fibula

Patella

Tibial tuberosity

Lateral
malleolus

The LATISSIMUS DORSI is shown transparently with the SERRATUS ANTERIOR partially lying beneath it.

The SERRATUS ANTERIOR is a flat sheet of muscle lying between the inside (ventral) surface of the scapula and the rib cage. Its origin is by fleshy digitations (fingers) from the upper eight or nine ribs which is the fixed point of the muscle. It is inserted along the whole inside vertebral border of the scapula. The digitations from the lower five ribs converge in the inner side of the inferior angle of the scapula and it is those which most concern the artist as they are seen so frequently. They appear as rich finger-like forms running at a slightly different angle than the ribs.

When the muscle contracts it pulls the more movable scapula forward around the rib cage. Because of the concentration of the muscle bundles at the inferior angle, it is this part of the scapula which is strongly rotated. The vertebral border and this inferior angle are landmarks to be looked for. They form the scapular shape while lying under the TRAPEZIUS and the LATISSIMUS DORSI. The SERRATUS ANTERIOR is used in pushing and punching actions when the arm (and the scapula) are brought forward, and in raising the arm above the head.

The EXTERNAL OBLIQUE is shown interdigitating with the digitations of the SERRATUS ANTERIOR. These little forms can often be seen at the area of intersection, with the shadow running downward and medially (to the midline).

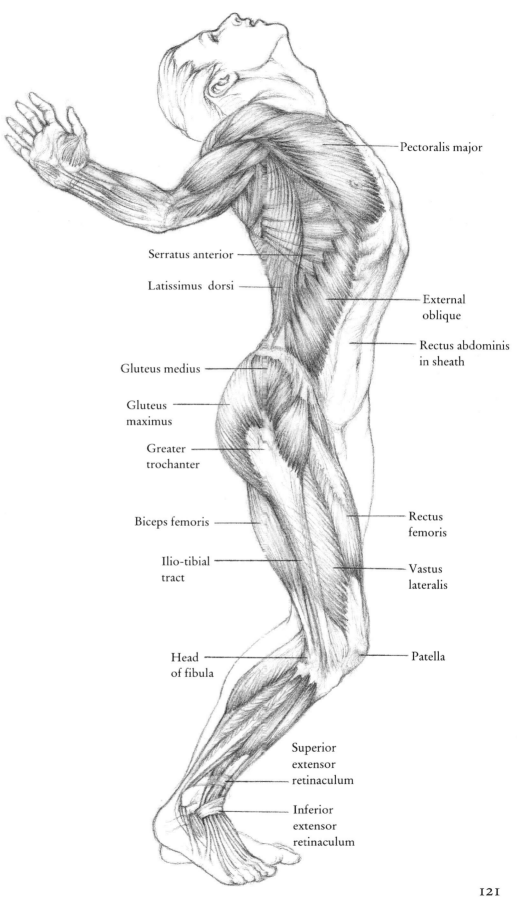

Pectoralis major

Serratus anterior

Latissimus dorsi

External
oblique

Rectus abdominis
in sheath

Gluteus medius

Gluteus
maximus

Greater
trochanter

Biceps femoris

Rectus
femoris

Ilio-tibial
tract

Vastus
lateralis

Head
of fibula

Patella

Superior
extensor
retinaculum

Inferior
extensor
retinaculum

A nude woman
Raphael, Sixteenth century
By courtesy of the British Museum

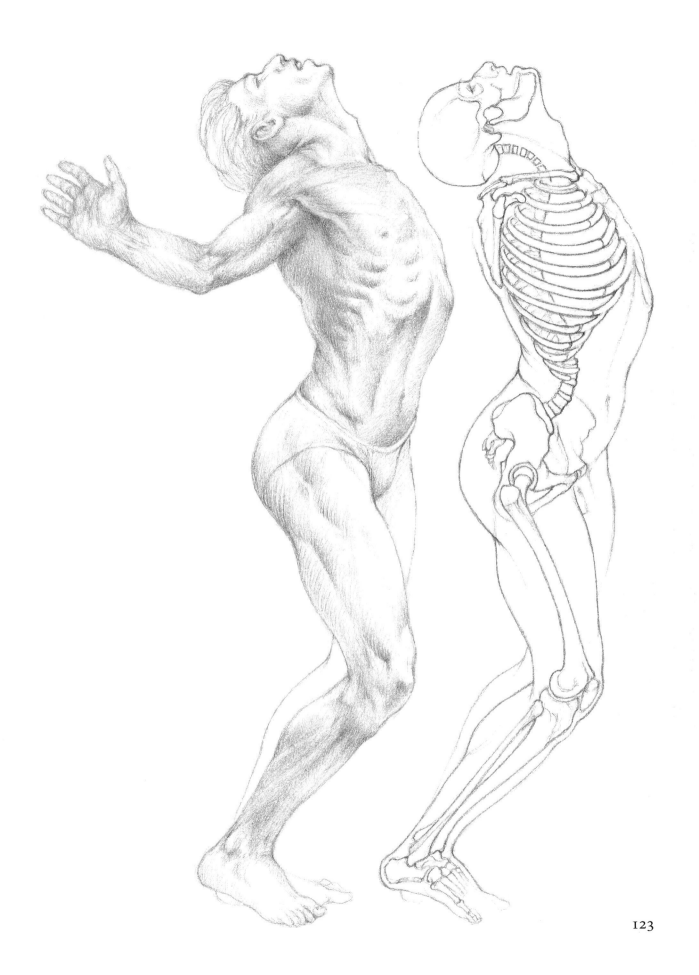

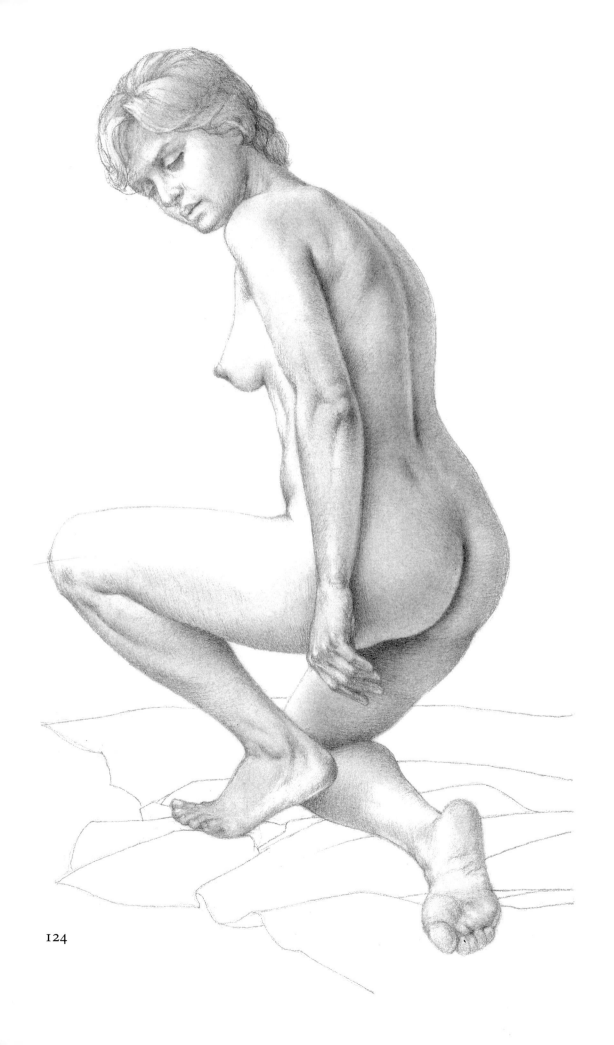

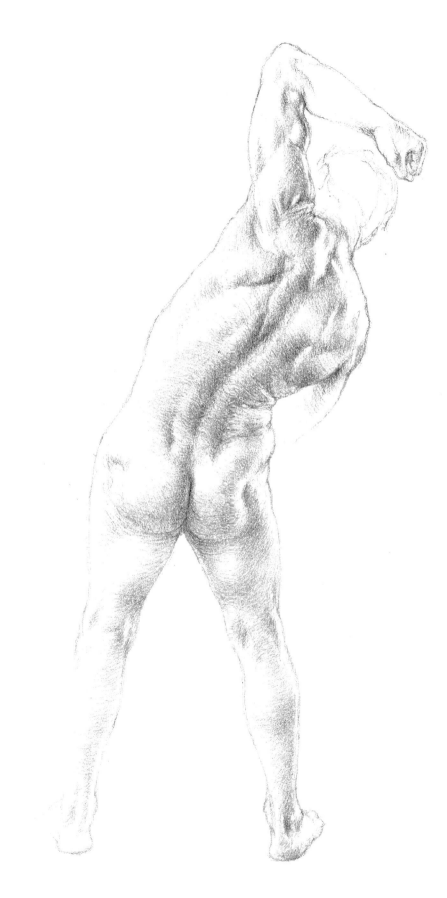

Index